First World War
and Army of Occupation
War Diary
France, Belgium and Germany

2 DIVISION
Divisional Troops
Royal Army Medical Corps
4 Field Ambulance
12 September 1914 - 31 December 1914

WO95/1336/1

The Naval & Military Press Ltd
www.nmarchive.com
Published in association with The National Archives

Published by

The Naval & Military Press Ltd

Unit 10 Ridgewood Industrial Park,

Uckfield, East Sussex,

TN22 5QE England

Tel: +44 (0) 1825 749494

www.naval-military-press.com

www.nmarchive.com

This diary has been reprinted in facsimile from the original. Any imperfections are inevitably reproduced and the quality may fall short of modern type and cartographic standards.

© Crown Copyright
Images reproduced by permission of The National Archives, London, England, 2015.

Contents

Document type	Place/Title	Date From	Date To
Heading	2nd Division Medical No.4 Field Ambulance Jan-July 1915		
Heading	4th F Amb Aug 1914		
Miscellaneous	Outline The Operation of II Field Ambulance	27/08/1915	27/08/1915
Miscellaneous	No. TV Field Ambulance Reserve From Guise To Meaux	17/12/1915	17/12/1915
Heading	2nd Division Medical 4th Field Ambulance Sep-Dec 1914		
Heading	No. 4 Fld Amble Sep 14		
War Diary	Oulchy-Vreny	12/09/1914	12/09/1914
War Diary	Vauxtin	13/09/1914	13/09/1914
War Diary	L of M	14/09/1914	14/09/1914
War Diary	Viel-Arcy	15/09/1914	16/09/1914
War Diary	Soupir	16/09/1914	06/10/1914
Heading	No 4. Field Ambulance Vol III		
Miscellaneous	2 Div	07/10/1914	07/10/1914
Miscellaneous	O.C.4 Fd Ambulance		
War Diary	Soupir	07/10/1914	12/10/1914
War Diary	Hopital	13/10/1914	13/10/1914
War Diary	Cassell	15/10/1914	15/10/1914
War Diary	Hazebrouck	15/10/1914	17/10/1914
War Diary	Boescheppe	18/10/1914	20/10/1914
War Diary	Vlamertinge	21/10/1914	21/10/1914
War Diary	Ypres	22/10/1914	27/10/1914
Miscellaneous	Military Hospital Ypres		
War Diary	Ypres	28/10/1914	29/10/1914
Miscellaneous	O.C.4 7a	28/10/1914	28/10/1914
Miscellaneous	No.4 Field Ambulance	28/10/1914	28/10/1914
War Diary	1 Mile W Of Ypres On The Ypres Vlamertinge Rd	30/10/1914	31/10/1914
Heading	No.4 Field Ambulance Vol IV		
War Diary	1 Mile W of Ypres on The Ypres Vlamertinge Rd	01/11/1914	03/11/1914
Miscellaneous	R.A.M.C. 2 Div Operating Orders	04/11/1914	04/11/1914
War Diary		04/11/1914	06/11/1914
War Diary	1 Mile W Of Ypres on Ypres Vlamertinge Rd	07/11/1914	08/11/1914
War Diary	1 Mile W Of Ypres	09/11/1914	16/11/1914
Miscellaneous	Operation Order By Col M. P. Holt A.D.M.S. 2nd Division		
War Diary		17/11/1914	17/11/1914
Miscellaneous	R.A.M.C. Operations Orders By Col M.P. Holt A.D.M.S 2nd Division	18/11/1914	18/11/1914
War Diary		18/11/1914	18/11/1914
War Diary	1 Mile N of Ypres	19/11/1914	20/11/1914
War Diary	Meteren	21/11/1914	30/11/1914
Heading	4th Field Ambulance Vol V Dec 1914		
War Diary	Meteren	01/12/1914	02/12/1914
Miscellaneous	Following Wire From 2nd Division	02/12/1914	02/12/1914
War Diary	Meteren	03/12/1914	13/12/1914
Miscellaneous	2nd Div Wire	13/12/1914	13/12/1914
War Diary	Meteren	14/12/1914	16/12/1914
Miscellaneous	2nd Divn Wires	15/12/1914	15/12/1914

Type	Location	From	To
War Diary	Meteren	17/12/1914	21/12/1914
Miscellaneous	Second Division	21/12/1914	21/12/1914
Miscellaneous	Reference To Wire	21/12/1914	21/12/1914
War Diary	Meteren	22/12/1914	22/12/1914
War Diary	Bethune	23/12/1914	25/12/1914
Miscellaneous	??		
War Diary	Bethune	23/12/1914	23/12/1914
Miscellaneous	O.C. No.4 Field Ambulance	24/12/1914	24/12/1914
War Diary	Bethune	25/12/1914	26/12/1914
Miscellaneous	No.4 Field Ambulance	26/12/1914	26/12/1914
War Diary	Bethune	26/12/1914	27/12/1914
War Diary	No.4 Field Ambulance	27/12/1914	27/12/1914
Miscellaneous	No.4 Field Ambulance	27/12/1914	27/12/1914
War Diary	Bethune	27/12/1914	28/12/1914
Miscellaneous	No.4 Field Ambulance	28/12/1914	28/12/1914
War Diary	Bethune	29/12/1914	29/12/1914
Miscellaneous	No.4 Field Ambulance	29/12/1914	29/12/1914
War Diary	Bethune	30/12/1914	30/12/1914
Miscellaneous	No.4 Field Ambulance	30/12/1914	30/12/1914
War Diary	Bethune	31/12/1914	31/12/1914
Miscellaneous	No.4 Field Ambulance	31/12/1917	31/12/1917
Miscellaneous	No.4 Field Ambulance	31/12/1914	31/12/1914
War Diary	Bethune	31/12/1914	31/12/1914

2ND DIVISION
MEDICAL

NO. 4 FIELD AMBULANCE

JAN - ~~DEC~~ JULY 1915

To Guards Div Aug 15

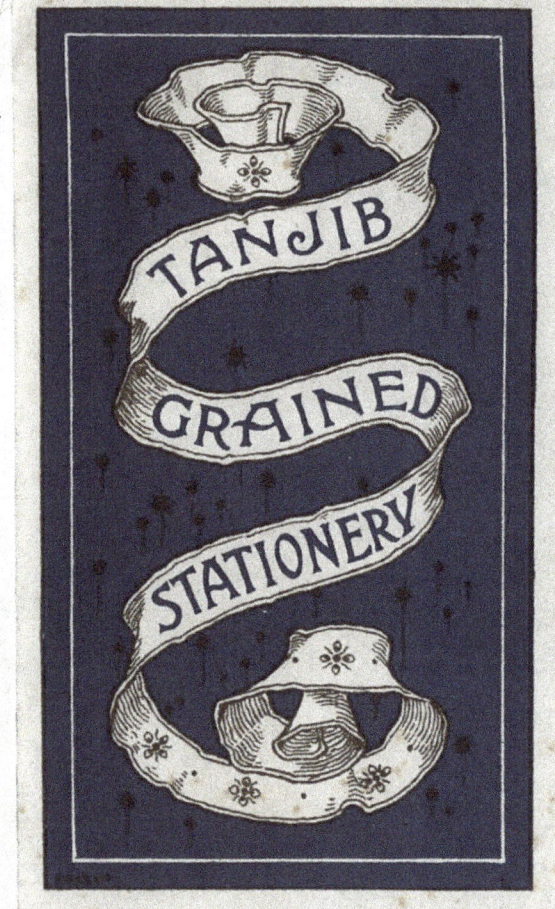

L⁴ Lamb
Aug 1914

Outline of the Operations of No II Field Ambulance during the Mons retreat 25/8/14 26/8/14 27/8/14.

———————————

The diary of a medical Field unit during active operations enables one to give a straightforward & unvarnished account of work carried out from time to time; & should also afford valuable information as to the utility or otherwise of our Standard equipment, personnel, unit formation, & the various items of previous organisation that either make for efficiency or for weakness, during the supreme test (actual) of warfare.

Unfortunately such a record could not be maintained for No 4 Field Ambulance during the great Mons retreat of 1914. And had it not been for the frequent appeals addressed to the writer

(2)

he would certainly never have attempted to record impressions from memory in regard to so important a matter. The story, then, is dependent upon ones own personal opinions and impressions formed during a period of great stress & many hardships.

3

We reached the village of GIVRY (towards the evening) 23/8/14 & parked our transport near the cross roads — at a point due north of ROUVEROY. I was second Senior Officer & had the command of C section. Orders were received to support the troops (including the 4th Guards Brigade), who had engaged the enemy at a not far distant point on the MONS Road — running N.W. from the village of GIVRY. As twilight fell, I was ordered to remain in position with my section, & the heavy transport of the unit; while A & B Sections, with a complement of Ambulances & stretchers, etc, went forward into action under fairly heavy fire.

4 (East)

the horizon to the north West, across a line with MONS itself as a central point, formed an unbroken glow of many fires as the enemy hords advanced, with their batteries in action.

My orders were to rapidly prepare the village of GIVRY for the greatest possible number of wounded, & attend to those returned from our advanced sections. A large barn was floored with straw, fires lighted nearby for the making of Bovril, etc, & the preparation of the dressing station completed with the utmost despatch. Lieut Routh, Rone, as Officer i/c of the station, worked strenuously, & unaided a force of fifty thousand.

About this time A & B sections rejoined & we retreated with the fighting troops via the road Quevy Le Petit, QUEVY LE GRAND, LA LONGUEVILLE, Pont-Sur-Sambre, to MAROILLES.

Meanwhile the Guards Brigade were, presumably, taking up their position on the LANDRECIES, MAROILLES front; but as no orders were, presumably, received by Major P.H. Collingwood, our O.C., since we were verbally directed to retire at GIVRY, & informed of the direction in which to proceed from that point, it was difficult to during the night, as the wounded were taken over, dressed, & even operated upon, when necessary to save life. In all, about 50 cases were received During this phase, with the assistance of the Village Maire & his people, further buildings were prepared; so that, by dawn, we could have received & fed some 1000 cases or more had they been transferred to the village. However, next morning 24/8/14, I received verbal orders from Col. H Thompson A.M.S., our A.D.M.S., to retire at once with my section, including the heavy transport

7.

State where our Brigade had taken up its defensive position prior to fighting the rear guard action of Landrecies.

So far as No IV Field Ambulance is concerned: we advanced due W from MAROILLES to a point on the main road one half mile or less from the Village of LANDRECIES. At that point a panic occurred.

Refugees — men, women, & children, detached troops and odd transport etc, etc, were stampeding towards us from LANDRECIES in utter disorder. We halted & rallied our men as best we could during the confusion. It was stated that the Uhlans had entered the Village of LANDRECIES. Two shots were then fired by the A.S.C. Ambulance drivers of our unit who "lost their heads". I would like to point out that these A.S.C. attached details should on no account have arms supplied to them. They do not understand their rifles, they utterly

8

neglect them; &, owing to lack of discipline as combatant soldiers, they are a positive danger to their own side. I would on no account issue rifles to them, even during Savage Warfare. Major Lynch Burne has since given me some interesting details as regards the panic above referred to. He obtained them from a German Officer whom he met when captured by the enemy after the Landrecies Affair. This officer stated that he had our unit under perfect observation during its progress along the Maroilles - Landrecie road; And that his men would have opened fire on us if the two rifles discharged by our drivers had injured any of his men. It appears that while the Guards were taking up their position across the Landrecies front the enemy had actually dug trenches across

9.

a cornfield & loop-holed a certain wall almost up against our troops. The natives of LANDRECIES had seen them, hence the panic; yet a patrol sent out by our division had failed to find any trace of the Germans so well were they concealed. This is the unsupported statement of a German officer. If true it would account for the panic, and the small number of enemy casualties which Major Lynch states he saw & counted after the action of Landrecies; & would also, perhaps, explain why the rifle fire was so heavy during the night of 25/8/14. owing to the close proximity of the opposing faces. Major Lynch also states that many of the British casualties on the night in question were due to our own fire.

10

but I cannot say what evidence he has for this conclusion.

To resume: Our O.C. halted his unit on the Maroilles Landrecies road about one half mile from LANDRECIES & took up his position in an adjoining field. Preparations were there made to receive wounded from an action that had begun, or was about to begin along our front. So far as I am aware we remained entirely out of touch with the Brigade of Guards during the night 25/8/14, although repeated efforts were made to effect communication with their staff.

During the night 25/8/14 a violent action developed; and about 12 pm the position of our ambulance became impossible owing to enemy fire in the immediate vicinity. In consultation with his Officers, Major Collingwood, having failed to effect a junction with the fighting line to any purpose, decided to fall back on the village of FAVRIL. This [retirement] was duly accomplished & the transport, with its horses still harnessed in, drawn up in line by the roadside running through FAVRIL.

Orders were apparently received towards Dawn 26/8/14 that the troops would retire along the main LANDRECIE LA GROISE road. No IV Field Ambulance therefore moved somewhat before daybreak & retired S.S.E along the minor road which joins the Landrecies La Groise main road at right angles one half mile to the north of La Groise. Accordingly at Dawn 26/8/14 No IV F Amb reached the cross roads one half mile N of LA GROISE & met the 2nd Division as it retired [in dense column] from Landrecies towards LA Groise, etc.

12.

was proceeded to join this column, but owing to the congestion of the road with troops & first line transport only A Section of the Ambulance succeeded in doing so. It therefore became detached from Sections B & C. Whose Ambulances & transport remained in line along the minor road running N N E to FAVRIL. I was therefore compelled to wait for a gap in the retreating column before proceeding further. This opportunity did not occur for 15 or 20 minutes; in fact it was impossible to march after A Section until the entire transport of 2 or 3 regiments had gone by. A Guards Regiment then passed the cross roads. One of their Senior Officers appealed to me for assistance. He stated that they had left behind some 160 wounded in a Convent School at Landrecies, about 3 miles back, but he could not say whether the enemy had as yet occupied the village or not. I hesitated for a moment as to what should be done; it was impossible, if the matter was organised regular medical personnel.

My detachment encountered small detached parties of our rear guard located about half way from our starting point on the LA GROISE, Landrecies road. No officer was seen with these troops & although we again passed them on our return journey, Major Lynch states that most of them were killed soon afterwards. We approached the village of LANDRECIES & found the road blocked with a barrier composed of Carts, barbed wire, and the trunks of trees, household furniture, and so forth. Our position appeared to be hopeless. After strenuous efforts in which all hands joined we succeeded in breaking through into the village

13.

to be taken in hand at all, to reach our OC who was already some distance away with A Section. The chances were against the heavy draught horses, with which the ambulances were drawn, effecting a successful & rapid 3 mile movement to the rear and out again with a convoy of wounded men. However, I decided to make the attempt. In the event of failure it would, of course, necessitate the loss of the ambulances & a couple of light field service carts from B & C Sections to the enemy, but not the heavy transport including A Section that was still complete on the road in front of us. I at once ordered six ambulances, 1 water cart, & a light medical store cart containing emergency equipment, into line & away at full speed towards LANDRECIES. Before leaving I sent a brief despatch to

Major P.A. Collingwood informing him of the facts & my present action. All heavy transport was likewise returned with instructions to rejoin A Section as soon as possible. I have since been informed by Major Lynch RAMC, who was then i/c of B Section, that our brigade Major - Major Ruthven Scott; Gds:- had, as a matter of fact, issued orders for the entire ambulance to return at once to LANDRECIES. I have no desire to comment on this order but must state my opinions under the circumstances. Fortunately for one I did not receive it. Had I done so I will go so far as to say that the entire unit would have passed into enemy hands & no wounded men could have been rescued from the LANDRECIES temporary hospital. To me it was as clear as daylight that those of us whom the enemy could capture, whether protected under the Geneva Convention or not, would <u>not</u> be returned to the British forces. Apparently our Combatant Commanders were not of this opinion, as I understand that they had already returned an enemy Cavalry F Amb complete to their foes. The manner in which our valuable medical personnel was frittered away at the beginning of this war can only be accounted for by want of appreciation, or knowledge & sense of proportion, on the part of those responsible. The advantage of clearing your wounded after an action is no less a tactical advantage because it is carried out on paper — under the Geneva Convention. That the enemy thoroughly understood this elementary fact was amply proved by their subsequent and successful efforts at depleting our highly trained, efficient & well

17

[(then) be discovered]
the Convent School full of Casualties.
Its interior
presented a scene that baffles description. The men were packed on the floors, some dead, others dying, with a proportion of "Walking" Cases. I reported my arrival to Major (W.B.) Fry RAMC. who was assisted by 4 or 5 other RAMC officers in doing all he could for this unfortunate mass of humanity.
It was soon apparent that

18

we should have to decide for ourselves as to how best to render assistance. Their Officers were worn out & so were their men.

I had 6 Ambulances available but not a moment to lose.

Fifty one Walking Cases, including 3 Officers, were packed into the waggons with the utmost despatch possible & the attempt to get them away begun.

As we left I met Major P H Collingwood with all his remaining Officers entering (the village) on horse back. He was briefly informed as to how matters stood; & agreed that I alone allowed continue any attempt to save this half Co of Guards, after which he & his party proceeded towards the Convent school with four Ambulances, a heavy waggon, & some of the light transport Cars.

Soon after this we met the remaining personnel of No 4. Field Ambulance and all its remaining heavy transport. Because Major Collingwood had already the balance of our empty Ambulances, & ample assistance as regards men from Major Fry's Unit, I decided, rightly or otherwise, to try & extricate our NCO's, men, and heavy transport together with the convoy of wounded already loaded on our waggons. I took this step deliberately believing as I did that, with the exception of the waggons our OC had with him, there was no other means available of removing any of the stretcher cases from the School before the enemy arrived. We had all the walking cases Major Loy could furnish. It would have been useless, I thought, to try & off load our medical supplies & use the heavy waggons for wounded.

case I estimated that time would not permit of our so doing. (Major Lynch states that this was our OC's intention) Further, distance considered, it appeared hopeless to attempt the removal of stretcher cases by hand with any prospect of success. Nevertheless Major Collingwood (apparently) thought something could be done.

When one half mile from the village I received a request from him for waggons. None were available for the reasons stated, yet such an appeal could not be ignored; &, much as I regretted doing so

22

I ordered (all) Our N.C.O's & men, with the exception of 1 N.C.O, 16 men, & the drivers with their 2 N.C.O's, under Sgt Major Ryan R.A.M.C, to return to the village & try to assist any comrades in their gallant attempt whatever it might be. [When about one mile & a half out I found a roadside farm & numerous churns of fresh milk. Despite the fact that every moment lost reduced our chances I advised all wounded men to drink as much of this milk as possible. They badly needed it; & as a further precaution

We piled up as many of the remaining Churns as our Waggons could carry on the tops of their loads. Lieut Hills RAMC joined us at this point with some information in regard from Major Collingwood, the substance of which I cannot remember.

He then returned towards LANDRECIES. Pte Gasmil RAMC, one of our cycle orderlies belonging to my section rejoined me shortly afterwards. He had been posted by me some way to our rear in order to observe the enemy; & now stated that a

German Motor Car, with staff officer, was on the road behind us; (that its occupants) had threatened to shoot Lieut Hills. Major Lynch states that this Car passed through LANDRECIES more than an hour before the German troops arrived.

We increased our speed as far as possible & came safely through the rear guard proper close to ETREUX some 9 miles from LANDRECIES.

With the exception of L⁺ & D. M. James RAMC, who left LANDRECIES, when I ordered the heavy transport away, all my brother officers and the personnel of No 4 Field Ambulance, save the details already noted, were Captured. We escaped some 30 Strong, & had all the heavy transport, (except one waggon belonging to A Section) 6 ambulances, 51 wounded, & most of the light Carts — water carts & med store carts — with horses complete.

25

About 1 mile south of LA. GROISE. We picked up Lt Nelson R.A.M.C. This officer (stated that he) had become detached from his regiment during the previous night. He was in a disshevelled & worn out condition, but after food & rest on one of our waggons, he proved valuable to the remenants of No 4 Field Ambulance in its work as a unit during the subsequent retreat.

26

From LANDRECIES we marched to ETREUX via LA GROISE. At ETREUX our convoy passed through the Guards Brigade entrenched in what appeared to be a strong defensive position. When we entered the village itself there was an impossible congestion of traffic there, & it was with some difficulty that I procured orders from a Staff Officer for the disposal of our wounded. We proceeded direct by main road to GUISE arriving at that point as night fell on 26/8/14 after completing a forced march of over 20 miles since dawn.

My men & horses were in dire need of food & rest. The convoy formed its bivouac, the wounded were dressed where necessary, & all hands supplied with a hot meal of sorts — after which they turned in.

Leaving Lt. Nelson in charge I proceeded to the Railway station of Guise, which was understood to be the next railhead for the retreating Army. Not a British Officer could be found but after searching the village I was at last fortunate enough to discover a French Officer. He stated that no train could be procured, but subsequently agreed to wire for one when the urgency (of our position) was pointed out to him. Before returning to Camp I arranged matters with the Maire.

We bedded down a large covered-in platform (at the station) with straw, & procured ample supplies of hot cocoa, coffee, & bread from the town.

The wounded were (then) moved to their new quarters, where they remained until the arrival of a train about 4 am, that carried them safely to the base for admission to Hospital.

On 27/8/15 the unit rested at Luise & rejoined its division which arrived there towards evening.

(1)

No IV. Field Ambulance.
Retreat from GUISE to MEAUX
"

This Unit marched with its Division for the first time, during the MONS retreat, from GUISE to (*?*) MONT D'ORIGNY.

The march was a comparatively short one of some 10 miles via the Guise Mont D'Origny Road. Billets were provided at MONT D'ORIGNY, a large Cart Yard nearby selected for the establishment of a Field Kitchen, & food prepared. The men had almost finished their evening meal when orders came to "prepare to move at a moments notice - enemy pressing in force"

2

The Transport pickets were posted & the remainder of the men ordered to turn in. Nothing unusual occurred during the night. Next morning the Division commenced to move off, yet no orders whatever had been sent to me!! We hurriedly packed our equipment, ascertained the proposed destination from a battery of Artillery as it moved away, & commenced our march.

Unfortunately no one remained in the unit who had any knowledge whatever of map reading, yet we were absolutely dependant upon our maps. There were two possibilities: either to read the map accurately & keep on the road; or, fail to do so, & fall into the hands of the enemy.

3

the latter misfortune had to be avoided at all costs. If we lost our ambulance the 4th Brigade of the 2nd Div: would have had no means of saving its wounded. Therefore we concluded that the following precautions were matters of urgent necessity (1) To afford all possible assistance to our sick & wounded

(2) Accurate map reading so that we might keep on the road with & in advance of our retiring division according to orders received.

(3) Judging from our experiences since the action at Landrecies, the staff responsible for issuing orders to us, were either too overworked, etc, or did not fully appreciate our value to the troops. In future we should ask

— 4 —

for Orders when possible — and, failing then, their receipt move without them.

(4) <u>The Horses & men must be fed as often as possible.</u> They were doing treble work & (one) never knew when the next opportunity for food would occur.

(5) <u>The Horses must be shod regularly</u> or they would fail us. Divisional arrangements for this service were unpractical.

(6) <u>All orders received</u> would be loyally attempted; but if found to be impossible we should not hesitate to ammend them to meet altered conditions, etc.

———//———

The above principles were carried out to the letter; & there can be no manner of doubt that they enabled us to complete the retreat, dispose of casualties

5.

in large numbers, & subsequently rejoi- -ed at SOUPIR
AISNE during the subsequent advance of the British forces.

From MONT D'ORIGNY to LA TERE. the retreat continued at high pressure. So far as this unit is concerned it is impossible to connect the details of various engagements, night marches, & operations generally, owing to the absence of records that could not be maintained under the circumstances. Even an admission & discharge book showed nothing save (chaos) owing to the mental condition of the NCO who was in charge of it.

Certain facts, however, so impressed one that they stand out as worthy of comment.

6

As regards the evacuation of our wounded to the Base: I sincerely trust that as a Corps we will never again agree to the impossible task that was forced upon us of trying to evacuate wounded without suitable transport. Admittedly the provision of horse transport for Field Ambulances was due to a compromise. Motor transport was too expensive for a public who did not believe in War, & still less in "Costly" preparation for its prosecution. What were the results? Our wounded were collected by the regimental stretcher bearers & carried to some central point for evacuation by the Field ambulance. (the ambulance) When it could be kept in view by its A.D.M.S. (or his staff officer) mounted upon horses instead of a motor car that was able to cover the distances in a reasonably short space of time. To expect any A.D.M.S. to do so without a motor car & during a retreat like this was sheer folly. When information as regards the location of wounded was received by us, heavy draught horses were available that, according to very stringent orders, "must not exceed a walk march" in speed. If by good fortune we secured our wounded, the next step was to find "refilling point": a point somewhere in the rear of the division, to which the A.S.C. heavy motor transport brought their food supplies; & from which their waggons started towards

8

railhead, located as it was some 20, 30, & 40 miles to the rear, with wounded & often badly wounded soldiers. The results were deplorable. The first function of a supply train is the feeding of its troops. Therefore, time is all important; & I prefer to avoid further comment as to what our wounded were subjected to, over roads of various quality, until they arrived at railhead. It is no exaggeration to say that it was a case of "the survival of the fittest"; & if the drivers of these waggons cared to tell their story (as they many times related it to me) our money grubbing public would be afforded plenty of material for arm chair criticism of the always popular Medical Corps "Scandals".

Yet we are, so far as one can ascertain, not entirely free from blame as regards the deficient medical transport furnished for the original expeditionary force.

It is said that proposals from us were always countered by the statement that "the presence of motors in the first line transport was impractical"

A first line must necessarily halt at frequent & uncertain intervals to conform to regimental movement; & motor transport, as a (matter of) fact, is unsuitable for the purpose.

The first line is not the place for a field ambulance. The best & only place for that unit

10

is "refilling point". From refilling point it can be deployed forwards, to a flank, or towards the rear; to an extent dependant upon existing circumstances & in detachments of suitable strength to any or all of these directions. The blunder of classing it as first line transport was one of the greatest errors we have made; & the excellent organization of our units proved a most unpopular hindrance to the Combatant Staff, owing to the occupation of their road space, or slow speed, obstruction to the regimental transport, & interference with the movements of

ASC supply trains that had perforce to await the arrival of wounded before starting for railhead.

So far as No 4 Field ambulance was concerned friction resulted between us & the Divisional staff. We naturally objected to being left behind the rear guard (time & again), working as a station, & without orders or information that the division was again retreating. It was certainly my duty to report such occurrences & protests were made from time to time. The result was slight improvement but reprisals of a personal nature against me, as the story will show.

In the absence of orders we depended upon the sound of moving transport as our signal to "pack up". We often had to find our own billets, or simply sleep on the roadside, and one therefore always tried to secure a position near the artillery whose movement warned us of a sudden departure. The field Ambulance of the future, or motor Ambulance Convoy-call it what you will - must exclude the horse at all costs. It may or may not be desirable to place horse drawn ambulances with the first line transport but they should be entirely apart from the Field Ambulance proper; & in my opinion their utility is very much open to doubt. A modern Motor Ambulance will cross any ground, over which it is advisable to move patients other than by hand, & its head quarters must be behind & not with the first line transport.

A word as to equipment. On one occasion I received orders to search a wood some 100 acres in extent for British wounded & my duties were to include "adequate attention to enemy wounded for which search should also be made". I had 16 worn out bearers available. The night was "pitch dark". That notorious article of equipment known as the "Bulls eye lamp" was therefore our "Guiding Star" — not to mention the regulation number of "Matches wax", that by this time were mostly expended examining road tracks by night at uncertain cross roads, & those that remained were soaked with water. This order was not complied with as we found more (British) wounded by the roadside than we could deal with. The provision of efficient electric torches should not have been overlooked during our peacetime preparations for war. Nothing could be more useless than the bulls eye lamp, a fact that was clearly demonstrated during the South African war, but apparently not so reported upon

15.

Our heavy transport was loaded up with much useless & unpractical equipment the weight of which on more than one occasion almost lost the unit to the enemy. Every item of equipment must be of the lightest & most portable description. It should be chosen by those of us who from <u>actual practical</u> experience in the field, especially during the Mons Retreat, know what is required & what is worthless. So far as equipment was concerned we simply dumped a quantity of the stuff by the roadside when its true value was apparent, retreated from it & were called up by letter as to "why a guard had not been mounted on our discarded stores"!!

At LA FÈRE the force crossed the river SERRE, blew up one span of the bridge imperfectly, & took up what appeared to be a strong position at CHARMES. Guns were "dug in", trenches completed & occupied, & the various preparations made to resist an expected attack by enemy forces. We were confident that we could hold them now & stop this demoralising retreat once & for all.

The remains of our unit then turned in for much needed rest while I personally remained on watch owing to an unusual & extraording sense of uncertainty. It was raining hard when about 10.30 P.m. a motor cyclist handed in a Chiv. "A French Reserve Division is retiring in some disorder on LA FERE AAA Prepare to move at a moments notice". The well known order "pack up" was cheerfully carried out by my unfortunate men, who at all events had been lucky enough to gain at least 2 hours sleep. Headquarters being close at hand I was able to obtain definite orders by personally waiting for them. etc. The Force retreated through the FORET. DE. GOBAIN by various roads.

18

During the entire retreat this was the most depressing night march we made. It was a dark night & so dark were the forest roads that one could scarcely see the outline of ones hand held at arms length.

So far as guidance was concerned we were fortunate in having obtained definite orders; but as we had no other unit near us our maps along saved the situation. Yet it was no easy task. Many of the matches were damp & the Bulls eye lamps worthless. We therefore expended our remaining matches with great caution — for map reading, and, as previously stated, for examining the road tracks at cross roads that confused us.

Fortunately for us the Divisional Second line transport had already retreated along this road so that its tracks were easily traced when our efforts on the map became uncertain. At one point even these methods failed us so Lt. Nelson knocked at a nearby cottage door in order to try & prove our direction. The French peasantry within were so terrified that some time elapsed before they would open their door & when they did so they professed no knowledge of the road that passed their wicket gate!! They apparently thought we were enemy troops!!!

20

The retreat was continued through SOISSONS & the Forest of VILLERS COTTERETS until we reached, I believe, the point Boursonne. Suddenly the division halted & prepared to resist attack from large enemy (Cavalry?) forces that were said to be pressing in towards us from the north western section of the Forest. Considerable confusion occurred on the road as our Artillery entrenched their guns towards the N.W. I saw one Regiment ordered backwards & forwards at least 4 times – it was a case of "order, counter order & disorder"

After some difficulty I persuaded the Combatant Staff Officer that our correct position was not side by side with the entrenched guns. He consented to the Ambulance moving to his left & rear flank, for about one half mile, in order to establish itself in a farm house & prepare a dressing station. Our arrangements (in this farmhouse) were about half completed when an artillery officer informed me that "we were located in the centre of his main position". I therefore moved to a nearby sugar factory which formed an admirable & well protected station towards which we arranged our direction flags from the Combatant line in front of us. In consultation with Major Bostock R.A.M.C., No 5 Field Ambulance, it was decided that he should retire with his unit to a railway station some 2 miles back, while our depleted unit acted, practically as a first aid station, in the sugar factory. This appeared to be the best arrangement under the circumstances & as a matter of fact worked admirably during the night. We passed through a large number of wounded during that night, having adjusted their dressings when necessary, checked haemorrhage of an urgent nature & supplied food & hot Bovril to the wounded. The casualties were certainly very heavy & we had worked as hard as it was possible for men to labour the night long.

In return we were left without orders in our position at day break, through the carelessness of the staff officer whose duty it was to issue instructions to retire with the Force.

At last he found us, &, by a strenuous effort on our part, we saved the unit once more before the enemy advanced scouts reached the position.

It was a narrow escape indeed, as we took the wrong road in error after leaving the sugar factory & had some difficulty in finding the correct route.

We eventually crossed the river Marne at a point some 3 or 4 miles West of ST JEAN. Then another incident occurred that almost landed us into the enemy as we crossed the River MARNE near LA.FERTE.
After crossing the River (Marne) we took a course due East & were about to turn South in accordance with our orders. At the cross road in question we were stopped by

a Senior N.C.O. who stated that he had the General's order to divert us to the next cross road turning south, "a very short distance on". It was an (on my part) error to take verbal instructions from anyone under the circumstances, but we had so often been forced to do so on previous occasions, that I now accepted the order as given in good faith. Altho I subsequently made a very thorough search for this NCO & failed to find him & cannot to this day say whether he was an enemy agent or not.

26

The result was that we did not discover our error until we had reached the village of St JEAN.

My horses were then urgently in need of water & food as were the men. A halt was ordered for this purpose as one had simply to take the risk at all costs. Had we possessed a motor unit the position would, of course, not have arisen; neither would other "mistakes" have occurred for which one receives a blame that was not merited from time to time.

The unit now returned with all possible speed W.S.W. from St JEAN & turned due W at the bend of main road under the word "Changis". At this point I met a Cavalry patrol whose commanding

Officer informed one that we were miles behind the Rear Guard & that he himself was out of touch with the Staff & without orders. I subsequently learnt that a whole battery of artillery had also been left behind in a certain field - unlimbered, in position, & without orders. Our horses were now pressed up some very steep hills with their already overloaded waggons & we reached MEAUX in due course & joined the Division.

While at MEAUX orders were received that the enemy was in retreat & that our forces would advance & attack forthwith. The advance proceeded N.N.E, during which our crippled unit did all it could to assist the wounded &

other ambulances (No V & VI) whose personnel was more or less complete. In this advance I was charged with "lagging behind" but the assumption was unjust as our condition was such that rapid movement, for the horses & men, could not be accomplished, even if we had been driven by an enemy behind us. On the contrary it is decidedly my opinion that we did all men could do under the circumstances, & we are content in that conviction & without further reward.

The CLIGNON river was crossed in due course & we established a dressing station where a considerable

number of casualties were dealt with at HAUTEVESNES. This station & its wounded were then handed over to another unit & our advance continued with the Division.
So far as I remember we passed LA CROIX, BRUERES, & FERE-EN-TARDENOIS but cannot state the exact roads traversed.
The AISNE region was now entered; &, at point 175 (under L of LONGUEVAL), towards the evening of a certain date, orders were received to billet in the village of St MARD, on the banks of the AISNE.
Our Ambulances, full of wounded,

followed the Irish Guards toward St MARD. Before we started it was fairly obvious that the village was untenable owing to enemy shrapnel fire; yet I received no contrary orders & was, for some reason unknown to me, allowed to proceed. As we approached the village the troops in front of us halted & their OC stated he did not intend to proceed further towards St MARD. The light was failing & something had to be done as regards our wounded. I reported to a Staff Officer who issued orders that we should return to point 175, & from that point take the road due W & S until we off loaded our wounded into an empty motor supply train that had orders to await our arrival 2 miles back or less. The point 2 miles back was reached without delay but no waggons were there. I ordered the unit to follow me up, & galloped forward towards BRAINE, to try & overtake the motor supply waggons that were now stated to have left for the BRAINE "some time ago". I found the supply waggons, under weigh, about 3 miles away from where I had parted from my unit; & after considerable difficulty stopped them to await the arrival of our wounded. The ambulance was moving very slowly so that

32

considerable time elapsed before its arrival. The delay referred to occurred in procuring a supply of straw for the wounded to lie upon. From previous experience I knew only too well what the motor supply waggons meant for a wounded man; & had left instructions that a good supply of straw must, somehow, be obtained & loaded on the tops of our ambulance waggons. They had secured the necessary straw but as the night was dark it was no easy matter to do so.

Further delay occurred owing to the congestion of the road where the supply waggons were; & without any assistance from the supply people I was compelled to move their waggons & mine, into various positions so that they could be prepared for my consignment of wounded. They were already almost full of casualties from elsewhere.

33

It was almost 11 P.m before we began our return journey.

What to do I knew not, as we were entirely without instructions nor had I any knowledge as regards the movements or position of the Division or what was required. Only one step suggested itself. It appeared to one advisable to establish the unit as a dressing station in a farm yard not far distant from point 175.

There we should at all events be prepared to take casualties from the front at daylight if no further orders were awaiting us. We halted by the roadside outside the farm in question; & for the first time since the retreat began my men appeared unwilling or unable to do more that night. The Horses were just able to draw their empty waggons & remain in an upright position as they had no rest & practically no food & water for many hours.

The men lay down by the roadside & were fast asleep almost before I entered the farm house. I then found a Cavalry Regiment in occupation & consulted its Commanding Officer as regards the proposed hospital. He said that of course he would clear out if I considered the place was absolutely necessary for wounded; but strongly advised me against remaining. I was told that the place would be swept by the enemy Artillery at daybreak & that there was no water there for the animals. He advised me to forthwith proceed to the village of COURCELLES, about 1½ miles E & S of the farm we were now in, & there halt until morning. He could not give me the information I required as regards the position of our Divisional Head quarters, etc. Something had to be done as regards our animals & personnel so I proceeded to billets in COURCELLES

35

The men were so worn out that they refused food & elected to sleep instead after they had attended to their horses.

Early next morning Staff Sgt Andrews ASC, the Senior NCO of our transport section, informed me that a move was out of the question unless shoes were provided forthwith for several horses who were now crippled through travelling with bare feet on the previous day.

The work was taken in hand without a moment's delay & some of our wounded who died during the night were buried.

It was 11 a.m. before we could leave the village towards point 175 again. We reached point 175 & there met Captain Davidson RAMC. our D.A.D.M.S. He stated that he had failed to find us on the previous evening when we should have crossed the river to Soupir & established there. That the General was extremely angry at our failure to do so etc etc

36

I now received orders to proceed towards VIEIL-ARCY, establish a temporary station at the point L'Hopital under Lt Nelson, & proceed with the waggons to a point immediately South of the Canal bridge at Pont-ARCY. This order was forthwith carried out. We established a temporary hospital in an empty farm at L'Hopital & to it transferred our wounded with Lt Nelson in charge. During the day I had 2 junior Lieuts R.A.M.C drafted to the unit. & these officers came forward with the transport.

The transport halted in a field immediately N of the road & close to the Canal bridge above referred to.

The men commenced to prepare their breakfasts & shortly afterwards a section of Artillery limbers came over the Canal bridge & passed up towards Vieil-Arcy. Scarcely had they done so when the enemy opened fire on us with their large ~~guns~~ Howitzer guns

I gave orders to retire in line. We continued to do so in good order for a short distance but the enemy had the exact range & continued a heavy fire that followed us up as we moved. When the unit broke in disorder, my groom cleared off on my horse, & it was some time before I could recover him & stop the stampede. While doing so a shell had blown up one of our horses & killed the driver of the waggon. Lt Howell Rome had a portion of his foot blown off & my mare was slightly wounded. Owing to the continued fire, I ordered the waggons into the temp hospital established nearby, in order to evacuate the wounded then into a place of safety — with all possible speed. Meanwhile I proceeded towards the canal bridge with the stretcher bearers & removed several casualties that were lying about the vicinity of the bridge. We also found the body of Lieut Armstrong RAMC who had been killed instantly by a large shell wound of the head. The entire road was littered with all kinds of artillery equipment, limbers, wounded horses, & human remains from the unfortunate battery that had endeavoured to use this road as we were leaving it towards the temporary hospital. We carried wounded from the Canal Bridge to the temp Hosp: our last patient - & hardly had we evacuated from that Building when the enemies guns found it & dropped several shells through the roof. They did this with a full knowledge of its function as we had a large red cross flag still flying in a position plainly discernable to their position. I would, however, like to add that it would have been an easy matter for them to destroy us as we returned

to pick up our casualties at the Canal
bridge but they respected our efforts
on that occasion & did not open fire.

It was now apparent that it would not
be possible to cross the AISNE at
PONT-ARCY as the Canal bridge, & the
pontoon over the river itself were both
under fire & impassable - for the present
at all events.

I was again stranded without orders & was
not aware of any other crossing available
for the unit to reach Soupir; nor did
I know what the intention was — whether we
should cross or not.
I did not know whether we were intended
as a reserve or otherwise. Presumably we
were a reserve to another ambulance that
had crossed; otherwise, why had we
received orders to park south of the
PONT-ARCY Canal Bridge within sight &
range of the enemies guns?

40

Accordingly I proceeded to VIEL-ARCY, ※ there established a temporary hospital, & handed over my wounded to Major [2nd in command] ——?—— who had already established a section of No V Field Ambulance in one of the buildings. A Report was at once sent to our ADMS Lt Col Copland R.A.M.C. giving full details of all that had happened to my unit from the moment we were compelled to retire from St Mard to date. I believe it was about midday on the following day when I received orders to proceed due east & cross the river AISNE by a pontoon bridge that had been established at OEUILLY. It was stated that the road from that point, via BOURG, to SOUPIR was under heavy artillery fire from the enemy guns but that I "must rush the waggons forward one at a time". There was considerable congestion

41

of traffic at the Pontoon Bridge so that it was 3 P.m., some 3 or 4 hrs after receiving the Order to move, before we reached the village of BOURG.

When we did so the streets were blocked with a Cavalry field Ambulance, Artillery & details of other units held up owing to the condition of the road in front. Wounded horses, various waggons with wounded drivers & cut up animals were struggling back from the direction of SOUPIR.

Lt. Nelson & I climbed to the top of a hill above the village of BOURG to inspect the road & see if it was possible "to rush the waggons forward one by one".

We could have done so with the absolute certainty of losing all our men & horses as the enemy had about 3 batteries in action & the road was quite impassable.

42

There was nothing for it except to halt until darkness set in. We moved at dusk & altho shelled at intervals along the road, which was now very congested with a moving division, SOUPIR was reached without a casualty.

The unit moved into the Chateau Soupir which had already been utilised by the regimental Medical Officers for their wounded. There was no shortage of dressings & such wounded as we found there had been well attended to, & so far as one could judge nothing more could have been done for them than was done pending our arrival — not a (dressing) required alteration. The Staff of a Cavalry division were occupying certain rooms in the Chateau but jo left the Building at my request.

43

We established a good hospital in the Chateau Soupir after a very few days & within one half mile of the nearest trench.

At my request the Supply Officer of the division despatched foraging parties every day. It was their duty to search the farms for & near for supplies. The result could not have been better & the food we procured in the form of milk, butter, eggs, vegetables, meat, poultry & so forth could not have been improved upon in any base Hospital — both as regards its quality & amount etc.

We had every facility as regards cooking in a large & splendidly appointed kitchen, an excellent operating room was fitted up, & wards arranged throughout the building.

The bedrooms of this Chateau were available not only for wounded officers but also for those who required a rest from the trenches & the advantages

of hot baths & good food in our
Mess etc.

The Hospital had been in operation about
one week or 10 days when I was ordered
to report myself to Divisional Head
Quarters to see the General

I was brought before the General Sir C Munro
& Severely reprimanded for neglect of
duty in not bringing the unit up to
time. He stated that he had read
my report & was not satisfied with
it: that during the retreat it had
taken all the time of one staff
officer to keep us on the road; and
that I had entirely misinterpreted the
Military Situation. No explanation or
defence on my part was permitted.

The work of refitting the unit was then
Carried out with all
despatch. The labour of preparing indent
wires & returns became very heavy; so
heavy indeed that I was Compelled

to take my Senior N.C.O. & three Clerks off their duties in connection with the sick & wounded & hospital (for clinical work & administration). Captain Lloyd Jones subsequently reported for duty with the unit as did a contingent of St Johns Ambulance men & various temporary Lieutenants. The work of repetition was almost complete when our A.D.M.S., Col Holt A.M.S. spoke to me as regards the Generals attitude. He suggested that it would, perhaps, be advisable under the circumstances to hand over the unit & asked me if I would care to do so. I agreed to his suggestion, was personally thanked by Br. Lord Cavan - Gds Brigade, for what we had accomplished for them & handed over command of the Ambulance to Capt Lloyd Jones RAMC.

London.
17/12/15.

W Lattan
Lt Col RAMC

2ND DIVISION
MEDICAL

4TH FIELD AMBULANCE

SEP - DEC 1914

TO GUARDS DIV

Nº 4 7ld Aube

Army Form C. 2118.

WAR DIARY
or
INTELLIGENCE SUMMARY.
(Erase heading not required.)

Instructions regarding War Diaries and Intelligence Summaries are contained in F. S. Regs., Part II. and the Staff Manual respectively. Title pages will be prepared in manuscript.

Hour, Date, Place	Summary of Events and Information	Remarks and references to Appendices
12-9-14 OULCHY-VIGNY	Reinforcements joined N° 4 Field Ambulance. Personnel Lieut APH Jones RAMC. (TS) Lieut Howell RAMC. (TS) and 65 NCO's men N° 17159 Sjt C Jones appointed A/S/m Marched to COURCELLES Billets there in houses late at night — very wet — *MKJ*	
13-9-14 VAUXTIN	Left Courcelles at 6.30 am marched to VAUXTIN. Delays on road. Lieut Lovell and one Australian mgr sent to collect wounded. At night bivouac'd at cross roads. Pickets Operating huts. 12 Cases admitted and attended to *MKJ*	

Army Form C. 2118.

WAR DIARY
or
INTELLIGENCE SUMMARY.
(Erase heading not required.)

Hour, Date, Place	Summary of Events and Information	Remarks and references to Appendices
14-9-14 2 P.M.	Advanced towards SOUPIR; but owing to being Shelled had to return beyond VIEL-ARCY. Owen Ludlow A.S.C. attached to the Field Ambulance was badly wounded and Lieut Howell was wounded in foot whilst attending him. Lieut Ludlow died later in the day. Whilst the convoy was still under shell fire a party of lancers under Major P.H. Falkner and Lieut. O'Neill collected wounded; these were brought to a farm and dressed; afterwards being conveyed by the Ambulances to near BRAINE, where they were transferred to motor lorries.	(sgd)

Army Form C. 2118.

WAR DIARY
or
INTELLIGENCE SUMMARY.
(Erase heading not required.)

Instructions regarding War Diaries and Intelligence Summaries are contained in F.S. Regs., Part II. and the Staff Manual respectively. Title pages will be prepared in manuscript.

Hour, Date, Place	Summary of Events and Information	Remarks and references to Appendices
15-9-14 VIEL-ARCY	A Dressing Station established at Viel-Arcy. A number of wounded were collected and transferred to motor lorries. Bivouac'd Farm House W. of Dressing Station.	
16-9-14 VIEL-ARCY	Left for BOURG at 2 pm over pontoon bridge the Bourg. Halted at BOURG, as the road beyond was under heavy shell fire. Proceeded at 6 pm. Slow progress owing to returning troops mostly cavalry & artillery. Arrived 8-45 pm in the yard of the Chateau of the CHATEAU SOUPIR.	

Army Form C. 2118.

WAR DIARY
or
INTELLIGENCE SUMMARY.
(Erase heading not required.)

Instructions regarding War Diaries and Intelligence Summaries are contained in F.S. Regs., Part II. and the Staff Manual respectively. Title pages will be prepared in manuscript.

Hour, Date, Place	Summary of Events and Information	Remarks and references to Appendices
16-9-14 SOUPIR	contd. Bearers were sent out and collected wounded from the trenches; these to the N.R.H. Hosp. were brought to the ambulance yard and transported by motor lorries to BRAINE. The last load left at 5.30 a.m. 17-9-14. MR9	
17-9-14 SOUPIR	Lieut J.M. Jones R.A.M.C. with 3 N.C.Os and 12 men F/Hospital with the heavy transport, but the 2 sections remained at the top. The CHATEAU SOUPIR was taken over and established as a dressing station. Promotion Affairs — Major P.H. Talbot R.A.M.C. Lieut. Nelson R.A.M.C. (R.O.) Lieut A.Y.H. Lowe R.A.M.C. (C.S.) MR9	
18-9-14 SOUPIR	Wounded = 86 A large number of German wounded prisoners were treated in the Church N. of the Chateau. Wounded = 63 MR9	

WAR DIARY
or
INTELLIGENCE SUMMARY.
(Erase heading not required.)

Army Form C. 2118.

Hour, Date, Place	Summary of Events and Information	Remarks and references to Appendices
19-9-14 SOUPIR	Casualties = 55.	
	6 Myers being Staff from dealing with the wounded	
	Sick received treatment were reestablished.	
	The R.A.M.C. personnel were killed over the stables	
	The A.S.C. horses near the horse lines.	
	Four Ambulance Wagons, 10 G.S. Wagons and one more	
20-9-14 SOUPIR	Carts were parked in front of stables; two Scotch	
	Carts in front of Chateau.	
	Casualties = 52	

Army Form C. 2118.

WAR DIARY
or
INTELLIGENCE SUMMARY
(Erase heading not required.)

Instructions regarding War Diaries and Intelligence Summaries are contained in F.S. Regs., Part II. and the Staff Manual respectively. Title pages will be prepared in manuscript.

Hour, Date, Place	Summary of Events and Information	Remarks and references to Appendices
21-9-14 Soupir	Casualties = 20	
22-9-14 Soupir	Casualties = 15. Lieut. Lowell left for duty with 1st Kings Liverpool Rifles accompanied by his father Lewis Andrew. Captain P.A. Shadforce R.A.M.C. arrived for duty.	

WAR DIARY
or
~~INTELLIGENCE SUMMARY~~
(Erase heading not required.)

Army Form C. 2118.

Hour, Date, Place	Summary of Events and Information	Remarks and references to Appendices
23-9-14 Soupir	Lieut N McH McCullagh. RAMC (SC) Lieut N Foot. RAMC C.S. Lieut B N Armstrong RAMC C.S. } Joined for duty Gunner. Newby. R.F.A. Casualties = 48. JMG.	
24-9-14 Soupir	Capt W.W. Boyce RAMC arrived for duty Casualties = 25. JMG	

Army Form C. 2118.

WAR DIARY
or
INTELLIGENCE SUMMARY.
(Erase heading not required.)

Instructions regarding War Diaries and Intelligence Summaries are contained in F. S. Regs., Part II. and the Staff Manual respectively. Title pages will be prepared in manuscript.

Hour, Date, Place	Summary of Events and Information	Remarks and references to Appendices
25-9-14 Soupir	Lieut H.A.P. Morton. R.A.M.C. (S.R.) and 1 N.C.O. and 70 men arrived for duty. Lieut Nelson left for H.Q for duty. Casualties = 55.	MKG
26-9-14	Revd D.H. Maggett (C.F.) with batman Pte Burr joined the Field Ambulance. Corpl Tophill from 2nd Divisional Train joined for duty. Casualties = 44	MKG

Army Form C. 2118.

WAR DIARY
or
INTELLIGENCE SUMMARY.
(Erase heading not required.)

Instructions regarding War Diaries and Intelligence Summaries are contained in F.S. Regs., Part II. and the Staff Manual respectively. Title pages will be prepared in manuscript.

Hour, Date, Place	Summary of Events and Information	Remarks and references to Appendices
27-9-14 Soupir	Casualties = 42.	
28-9-14 Soupir	Casualties = 32. Rev? 7/ Fleming (C.F.) with Batman Private Lawrence joined.	MG
29-9-14	Casualties = 17. The Church-yard was used as a cemetery & a plan showing position of the graves was kept.	MG

Army Form C. 2118.

WAR DIARY
or
INTELLIGENCE SUMMARY.
(Erase heading not required.)

Instructions regarding War Diaries and Intelligence Summaries are contained in F.S. Regs., Part II. and the Staff Manual respectively. Title pages will be prepared in manuscript.

Hour, Date, Place	Summary of Events and Information	Remarks and references to Appendices
30-9-14 Soupir	Casualties = 13	PKG
1-10-14 Soupir	Casualties = 22	PKG
2-10-14 Soupir	Casualties = 20	PKG
3-10-14 Soupir	Casualties = 31. Lieut B.W. Armstrong. Came (6S) left for Rhingo Lyons. rejt for duty	PKG

Army Form C. 2118.

WAR DIARY
or
INTELLIGENCE SUMMARY.
(Erase heading not required.)

Instructions regarding War Diaries and Intelligence Summaries are contained in F.S. Regs., Part II. and the Staff Manual respectively. Title pages will be prepared in manuscript.

Hour, Date, Place	Summary of Events and Information	Remarks and references to Appendices
4-10-14 Soupir	Casualties = 10 Lieut A.G.H Lord wounded from 1st Kings Royal Rifles for duty.	PKR9.
5-10-14 Soupir	Casualties = 2.6. 6th Infantry Brigade establishes position over Stables at Chivres	PKR9.
6-10-14	Casualties = 12 Weather good	PKR9.

No 4. Field Ambulance.

Vols II & III

Copy

DADMS
2 Div.   7-10-14

In accordance with your instructions
Major P.H. Falkner RAMC has
handed over 4th Field Ambulance to
Capt P.A. Lloyd-Jones RAMC, and
tonight proceeds to destination
AAA

From OC 4th Field Ambulance
Soupir
8.15 pm

Copy –

Serial No.   Date
O.C. 4 F. Ambulance.   MD303A.   24th

The Bearer Subdivision of No.6 Field Ambulance will proceed to road junction between 2 and 3 kilometre point YPRES-ZONNEBEKE ROAD and take up a position at S.E. corner of road junction. The ambulance wagons of No.6 Field Ambulance now at farm N of 3 kilometre point YPRES-MENIN (GHELUVE) Road will proceed to the above position. Sites for dressing stations in the neighbourhood should be noted.

Bearer Subdivisions of 4 and 5 F. Ambulances at present at Fm N of 3 kilms point YPRES-MENIN (GHELUVELT) Road will remain in present positions together with ambulance wagons of 4 Fd Amb; the Bearer Sub Division 4 Field Amb to be held in reserve.

Casualties will be evacuated to 6 Fd Amb Episcopal College YPRES.

HQ 2 Div
2.15 pm   Signed J.J. Irvine
                                    Maj
                           DADMS 2 D.

Send two mounted officers each from
No 4 F.A. & from 5 F.A. also one
mounted officer from 6 F.A.
Meet me there as soon as possible
4th & 5th Inf Brigades are up in
firing line. 6th Bde in reserve just
N.E. of YPRES

Signed M.P. Holt
Col
HdQrs II Div   ADMS
St Julien
  10.50 am

Army Form C. 2118.

WAR DIARY
or
INTELLIGENCE SUMMARY.
(Erase heading not required.)

Hour, Date, Place	Summary of Events and Information	Remarks and references to Appendices
7-10-14 SOUPIR	Captn P.A. Lloyd-Jones R.A.M.C. took over command of 4th Field Ambulance. Major P.H. Falkner R.A.M.B. left for duty at the Rover. No.13075 Pte Donne H.R. Brone left for duty at Rover. The wounded are placed in caves about one mile wholly away from the CHATEAU SOUPIR, where we have our dressing station, and are treated there by the Medical Officers in charge of regiments. Ambulance Wagons are sent out after dark to collect them. Shrapnel are continually bursting in the woods about 600 yards away; but only occasional pieces of casing fall near the CHATEAU. Number of casualties - 22 No. 5 Field Ambulance at Vieil-ARCY Personnel: Officers 8 Rank and file 175. A.S.C. 44. One W.O. and 10 S/Sergts - Sergts short of establishment	

Army Form C. 2118.

WAR DIARY
or
INTELLIGENCE SUMMARY.
(Erase heading not required.)

Instructions regarding War Diaries and Intelligence Summaries are contained in F.S. Regs., Part II. and the Staff Manual respectively. Title pages will be prepared in manuscript.

Hour, Date, Place	Summary of Events and Information	Remarks and references to Appendices
8-10-14 SOUPIR	Visit from A.D.M.S. 2nd Division who is at BOURG. Number of casualties = 16 Lieut. E H MOORE R.A.M.C. (S) arrived for duty. No 3693 Pte Dale J. Param Band. to R. Burke for duty No 19986 Corpl Gardner N Ramb Joined for duty from 1st R Berks No 4949 Corpl Tuson L Ramb Joined for duty from 70 MBatty R.F.A.	

WAR DIARY
or
INTELLIGENCE SUMMARY.
(Erase heading not required.)

Army Form C. 2118.

Hour, Date, Place	Summary of Events and Information	Remarks and references to Appendices
9-10-14 SOUPIR	The CHATEAU has three storeys; the first floor rooms are now for sick Officers; On the ground floor there are:- (1) A Medical Inspection Room (2) Clerks department in Hall (3) One dressing room (4) Operating room (5) Wards for wounded (6) Wards for sick (7) Kitchens used for cooking for Officers R.A.M.C. and sick Officers. In the basement there is a large room, previously used as a Chapel; into this are put some lightly wounded cases, who are returned to their regiments, and men who are suffering from sickness which is not acute. An isolation ward for Enteric Fever cases is formed under the tricps outside the front door of the CHATEAU. All the lower floors, so I hand in numerators. RLQ	

WAR DIARY
or
INTELLIGENCE SUMMARY.

Army Form C. 2118.

Hour, Date, Place	Summary of Events and Information	Remarks and references to Appendices
9-10-14 SOUPIR	cont-d An isolation ward for other infectious diseases is formed in a room in the stables. The NCO's and men of the Unit are accommodated in the stable building, behind the Office of the 4th Guards Infantry Brigade. Trench Latrines, incinerators and catch pits are always used by this Unit. The wounded sick are evacuated by means of Horsed Ambulance Wagons. Via the pontoon bridge to BRAINE, from where they are taken to HOPITAL. This evacuation is carried out after dark. Evacuation = 20. The plant of the electric lighting was overhauled by an officer of the 16 B.S. and is in working order. All officers NCO's & men of my unit serving at SOUPIR were inoculated against enteric fever. PTO	

Army Form C. 2118.

WAR DIARY
or
INTELLIGENCE SUMMARY.
(Erase heading not required.)

Instructions regarding War Diaries and Intelligence Summaries are contained in F.S. Regs., Part II. and the Staff Manual respectively. Title pages will be prepared in manuscript.

Hour, Date, Place	Summary of Events and Information	Remarks and references to Appendices
10-11-14 Soupir	The village of CYS was heavily bombarded yesterday. N° of casualties = 36	MG9
11-11-14 Soupir	N° of Casualties = 21	MG9

WAR DIARY
or
INTELLIGENCE SUMMARY.
(Erase heading not required.)

Army Form C. 2118.

Hour, Date, Place	Summary of Events and Information	Remarks and references to Appendices
12-10-14 SOUPIR	N° of casualties at SOUPIR during period from Sept 16 to Oct.12/14 = 1038. All evacuations were turned out after dark. Left SOUPIR at 11pm for HOPITAL and slept there. Personnel & Transport accommodated in field & farm houses at Viel Arcy. The weather here has been good while at SOUPIR. During the period at Soupir the Quarter Master remained at L'Hopital and supplies obtained by him daily at refilling point were forwarded by night to SOUPIR	
13-10-14 HOPITAL	Started at 8 pm for FISMES, where Unit entrained for CASSELL	MS9 MS9
15-10-14 CASSELL	Arrived at Cassell at 7 am. Breakfast at Station. Pte Everett reported sick & evacuated. Marched to HAZEBROUCK.	MS9

WAR DIARY
or
INTELLIGENCE SUMMARY.
(Erase heading not required.)

Army Form C. 2118.

Hour, Date, Place	Summary of Events and Information	Remarks and references to Appendices
15-10-14 HAZEBROUCK	Cont'd Personnel billeted in Schools. Officers of Unit in RUE-DE-MERVILLE Transport in Church Enclosure Officers of Unit Capt P.A. Lloyd-Jones R.A.M.C. Capt W.W. Boyce R.A.M.C. Lieut H.H.P. Morton R.A.M.C. Lieut A.G.H. Lovell R.A.M.C. Lieut W. Foot R.A.M.C. Lieut W. McH. McCullagh R.A.M.C. Lieut E.H.H. Moore R.A.M.C. Lieut G.M.L. Jones R.A.M.C. Attached:- Revd H.J. Fleming (C of E) Father P.M. Waggett (C of E) N° of Sick = 8.	

Army Form C. 2118.

WAR DIARY
or
INTELLIGENCE SUMMARY.
(Erase heading not required.)

Instructions regarding War Diaries and Intelligence Summaries are contained in F.S. Regs., Part II. and the Staff Manual respectively. Title pages will be prepared in manuscript.

Hour, Date, Place	Summary of Events and Information	Remarks and references to Appendices
17-10-14 HAZEBROUCK	Marched away at 7 am from HAZEBROUCK, proceeded via ST SYLVESTRE - STEENVOORDE - to BOESCHEPPE leaving POPERINGHE on the left. N° of Sick - 4. Billeted in Curé's house at BOESCHEPPE. Hospital in Monastery Girls' School. N° of Sick - 4	PMG.
18-10-14 BOESCHEPPE	The following men were appointed altogether to facilitate the letter writing of the three sections and to fill the appointments of the number of N.C.O. N° 14293 Happy Pte Eaton. N° 17929 Pte Blenkin. N° 3169 Pte Agnew 3145 Pte C. mahn " 3156 Pte T. Dair. 12656 Pte J. McKeown. 7266 Pte J.E. McNeill. RMO. " 9063 Pte G.N. Marcell. 14660 Pte L. Pack. 3158 Pte R. Steele 17043 Pte master 3771 Pte J. mott 12341 Pte J. P. cannon Reis? Day temporarily transferred from the 5th to 6th Field Ambulance for duty.	PMG.
19-10-14 BOESCHEPPE	Lieut E.A. Moore R.A.M.C. (C.S) proceeded to 41 N. Batt'y. R.F.A. for duty	PMG

WAR DIARY
or
INTELLIGENCE SUMMARY.
(Erase heading not required.)

Army Form C. 2118.

Hour, Date, Place	Summary of Events and Information	Remarks and references to Appendices
20.10.14 BOESCHEPPE.	Left Boescheppe, proceeded via HERZEELE-VLAMERTINGE. No 4 Field Ambulance, was passed on the road. Billeted in Town Hall and surrounding houses. Rain fell on the way. Ward for sick on first floor of Town Hall. 8 sick evacuated on British Supply A.S.C Motor lorries.	
	Corpl. Coad and two men were left at BOESCHEPPE with sick until they could be taken away by Clearing Hospital.	
	The NCO & men proceeded afterwards to POPERINGHE and reported at CHATEAU 1 mile W of YPRES on VLAMERTINGE Road 10 days later.	
	Capt. T.S. BLACKWELL RAMC. reported his arrival for duty and assumed command of B Section.	P.M.O.
21.10.14	Lieut G.E. DYAS. RAMC. arrived for duty	P.M.O. P.M.O.

Army Form C. 2118.

WAR DIARY
or
INTELLIGENCE SUMMARY.
(Erase heading not required.)

Hour, Date, Place	Summary of Events and Information	Remarks and references to Appendices
21-10-14 VLAMERTINGHE	Lieut N. Foot R.A.M.C. (CS) proceeded to 3rd Coldstream Gds. for duty. N°5 and 6 Field Ambulances here. Left for YPRES and arrived opposite Town Hall at 10-30 am. Took over School of Music and Boys & Girls Schools in RUE-DES-CHIENS. Made 500 beds — Mattresses and covers procured in town and stuffed with hay got by requisition — Acetylene lamps procured in town: When iron bedsteads from French in exchange for mattresses. Covers. Heavy Rain. Casualties = 263. Over received this morning for heavy division to proceed from VLAMERTINGE to ST JULIEN via WILTJE and their establish an advanced dressing station in the School rooms. Later they proceed to a farm 3 kilometre point on YPRES-MENIN R° N of YPRES. While at the last named place they had small advanced dressing station on a track 5 kilometre point on YPRES — MENIN R? Wounded brought in from hearers by horsed Ambulance.	

WAR DIARY
or
INTELLIGENCE SUMMARY.
(Erase heading not required.)

Army Form C. 2118.

Hour, Date, Place	Summary of Events and Information	Remarks and references to Appendices
22-10-14 YPRES	Lieut T.L. Hardi. R.A.m.b. (CS) and Lieut A.R. Esler Camb. (CS) arrived for temporary duty. N° of Casualties - 55. N°s 5 + 6 Field Ambulance have opened dressing stations at YPRES. Very cold weather.	mg.
23-10-14 YPRES	N° of Casualties - 86.	mg.

WAR DIARY
or
INTELLIGENCE SUMMARY.
(Erase heading not required.)

Army Form C. 2118.

Instructions regarding War Diaries and Intelligence Summaries are contained in F.S. Regs., Part II. and the Staff Manual respectively. Title pages will be prepared in manuscript.

Hour, Date, Place	Summary of Events and Information	Remarks and references to Appendices
24-10-14 YPRES.	No of Casualties = 64. Extract from Corps Orders:- No 10577 Sergt. J. Tovie to S/Sergt 12/14 " 237 Pte J.G. Hewell to be Cpl 20/14 " 5050 Pte W. Burntwhistle to be Corp 12/14	OM9
25.10.14 YPRES	No of Casualties = 42. Revd J. Bursley. (R.C.) arrived for duty. Revd Father Day proceeds to 5th Field Ambulance for duty (Relieves No 300 Pte J. Kerr 3 Hussars joined for duty (listener to Revd J. Bursley)	OM9

Army Form C. 2118.

WAR DIARY
or
INTELLIGENCE SUMMARY.
(Erase heading not required.)

Instructions regarding War Diaries and Intelligence Summaries are contained in F.S. Regs., Part II. and the Staff Manual respectively. Title pages will be prepared in manuscript.

Hour, Date, Place	Summary of Events and Information	Remarks and references to Appendices
26-10-14 YPRES	N° of Casualties = 129 N° 17991 Gunnr H. Nesby admrn to Convt Hosp. 26/10 N° 1067 Private Donald Rimb. to Hospital 26/10 N° 3693 Private W. Furness RAMC to Hospital 26/10	MQ. MQ
27-10-14 YPRES	N° of Casualties = 58	

Copy –

Military Hospital
YPRES

Sender's Number   Date
SC 765   28th

Prince Maurice of Battenberg's body is sent in by ambulance to-night AAA Please take it over and inform 1st Army Corps H.Q. who will make arrangements for coffin and despatch of body home.

MG

From 6th Inf Bde

3-5 am

WAR DIARY
or
INTELLIGENCE SUMMARY.
(Erase heading not required.)

Army Form C. 2118.

Hour, Date, Place	Summary of Events and Information	Remarks and references to Appendices
28-10-14 YPRES	No. of Casualties = 30. Total Casualties = 727 in YPRES. Casualties evacuated by Motor Ambulances to Railway Station and thence proceeded by Ambulance Trains. Weather changed - from Rain. MAG	
29-X-14 YPRES	Left YPRES at 3pm after handing over buildings to No. 3 Clearing Hospital, and proceeded to CHATEAU 1 mile N of YPRES on the YPRES-YLAMERTINGE Road). MAG	

Copy

Sender's No.   Date
G.M.21   28-10-14

OC 2 F.A.

Dispositions for 29th will be precisely same as today with the exception that in Sect A Bearer Subdivision of each F.A. will be required — & positions will be taken up by 10 am. Remaining Bearer Subdivisions will remain in reserve at respective tents.

NB Bearer Divn of No 4 F.A. is now billeted at same farm as No 5 Bearer Dn N of 3K YPRES – MENIN Road

            Signed M P Holt
            Col
From Hq   ADMS
   II Dn
7-15 pm

Copy

No. 4 Field Ambulance
After handing over to Clearing Hospital proceed with your Field Division to 1 Kilometer W. along YPRES-POPERINGHE Road AAA Report when handing over is complete and also upon arrival at destination noted above

2nd Echelon   Signed H Devine
H.Q. 2nd Division   Major RAMC
25·X·14   ADMS 2 Div

A.D.M.S.   *Copy*
2 Division   25-10-14
Have handed over buildings on Rue des CHIENS to O.C. No 3 Clearing Hospital AAA Am now proceeding to Chateau 1 Mile W. of YPRES on VLAMERTINGHE Rd AAA

       O.C. 4th Field Ambulance
       2·40 PM

Army Form C. 2118.

WAR DIARY
or
INTELLIGENCE SUMMARY
(Erase heading not required.)

Hour, Date, Place	Summary of Events and Information	Remarks and references to Appendices
30-10-14 1 Mile W of YPRES on the YPRES - VLAMERTINGE Rd	Went in to YPRES to help O.C. 6th Field Ambulance at EPISCOPAL COLLEGE. NCO's and men slept at COLLEGE. M.O's did duty in reliefs during night Enemy started to shell the Town in the night. Lieut F.C. MacDonald R.A.M.C. (CS) arrived for duty. Weather Cold "Henry Sam" MMG	

Army Form C. 2118.

WAR DIARY
or
INTELLIGENCE SUMMARY.
(Erase heading not required.)

Instructions regarding War Diaries and Intelligence Summaries are contained in F. S. Regs., Part II. and the Staff Manual respectively. Title pages will be prepared in manuscript.

Hour, Date, Place	Summary of Events and Information	Remarks and references to Appendices
31-10-14 1 Mile N of YPRES on the YPRES-VLAMERTINGE Rd	Opened Dressing Station at CHATEAU. Made 200 beds. Lightly wounded and sick on the first floor. Severely wounded on ground floor. Bivouac for walking cases where not actually sick in front of house. No. of casualties = 114 Bearers now at S.W. corner of ZILLEBEKE LAKE at road angle. No 5 & 6 Fd Ambulances at YPRES. Dispensed with tents early in operations (except 1 Operating Shut) night stools, fillers... Mater developed & chlorine in water carts. Very heavy rains MRJ	

Ans

No 4 Field Ambulance.

Vol IV.

WAR DIARY
or
INTELLIGENCE SUMMARY.
(Erase heading not required.)

Army Form C. 2118.

Instructions regarding War Diaries and Intelligence Summaries are contained in F.S. Regs., Part II. and the Staff Manual respectively. Title pages will be prepared in manuscript.

Hour, Date, Place	Summary of Events and Information	Remarks and references to Appendices
1-11-14 1 Mile N of YPRES on the YPRES-VLAMERTINGHE Rd	Wounded evacuated by Motor Ambulances to POPERINGHE thence by Ambulance Train to BOULOGNE. Numbers on reception (sick wounded) sent to hospital at 1pm & 6 pm and Admits at 8 am daily No 6384 Pte N Hall to Hospital Base Casualties = 31.	MRG

Army Form C. 2118.

WAR DIARY
or
INTELLIGENCE SUMMARY.
(Erase heading not required.)

Instructions regarding War Diaries and Intelligence Summaries are contained in F.S. Regs., Part II. and the Staff Manual respectively. Title pages will be prepared in manuscript.

Hour, Date, Place	Summary of Events and Information	Remarks and references to Appendices
2-11-14 1 Mile N. of YPRES on YPRES-VLAMERTINGHE Road	No 6398 Capt. Ernst Fanshaw'S to No 6 Field Ambulance No of Casualties = 71	

WAR DIARY
INTELLIGENCE SUMMARY

Army Form C. 2118.

Hour, Date, Place	Summary of Events and Information	Remarks and references to Appendices
3-11-14	Casualties:- 4.9. No 8135 Pte H. Fitch R.A.M.C. } Returned from Hospital No 3615 Pte M. Costello R.A.M.C. } Base. No 14815 Pte Jones.R. No 18438 " Boyce L. No 3462 " Edwards M. } Joined for duty No 3883 " Neary J. No 3594 " Smith M.	PMLS

Copy

R.A.M.C. 2 Div Operating orders
by Bt Col M.P. Holt DSO. ADMS 2nd Div

1. Moves

The Tent Divisions of Nos 5 and 6 Field Ambulances when cleared of Sick & Wounded will vacate their present dressing Stations in YPRES. They will proceed to the area between Y-VLAMERTINGE and Y-DICKEBUSCHE Roads and take up a position convenient to the former road. They will remain parked until further orders. Notification will be sent to ADMS. as soon as possible describing position taken up.

2. Sick & Wounded

Sick & wounded will be conveyed by Bearer Divisions to Dressing Station of Nº 4 Fld Amb at Chateau 1 mile W of YPRES on Y-VLAMERTINGE Road. Evacuation should take place as soon as possible from Nº 4 F.A. Dressing Station to POPERINGHE in order that there may always be accommodation for fresh cases.

3. Distribution of Bearer Divisions

Nº 4 F.A. Advd Dressing Station with Lord Cavan's Bde. KLEIN ZILLEBEKE

Bearer Sub Divn" in reserve at ZILLEBEKE

No 5 F.A. Advd Dressing Station — consisting
1½ B. Sub Div and 2 Amb: Wagons at
White House nr ZONNEBEKE — Remainder
in reserve at S side of Y-ZONNEBEKE Rd
2½ Km from YPRES.

No 6 F.A. Advd Dressing Station, consisting of
1 Section at 5 Km pt YPRES-MENIN Road
Remainder in reserve at Farm N of 3 Km
pt YPRES-MENIN Rd.

Position of ADMS and DADMS.

ADMS at reporting centre 2 Divn HQ nr Farm
2¾ Km from YPRES on Y-ZONNEBEKE Rd
South Side. DADMS at Episcopal College Y.

Signed J S Irvine
Major
DADMS 2nd Divn

4-XI-14

Army Form C. 2118.

WAR DIARY
or
INTELLIGENCE SUMMARY.
(Erase heading not required.)

Instructions regarding War Diaries and Intelligence Summaries are contained in F. S. Regs., Part II. and the Staff Manual respectively. Title pages will be prepared in manuscript.

Hour, Date, Place	Summary of Events and Information	Remarks and references to Appendices
4-11-14	Guerulles :- 139	PXq.

WAR DIARY
INTELLIGENCE SUMMARY.

(Erase heading not required.)

Army Form C. 2118.

Hour, Date, Place	Summary of Events and Information	Remarks and references to Appendices
5-11-14	Visit from Duchess of Sutherland who took away 10 wounded to POPERINGHE in her Motor Ambulance. "Croix de Guerre chleri" - 187. No 3462 Pte Edwards CAMC to Hospital Base.	1919

Army Form C. 2118.

WAR DIARY
or
INTELLIGENCE SUMMARY.
(Erase heading not required.)

Instructions regarding War Diaries and Intelligence Summaries are contained in F. S. Regs., Part II. and the Staff Manual respectively. Title pages will be prepared in manuscript.

Hour, Date, Place	Summary of Events and Information	Remarks and references to Appendices
6-11-16 Beauval	:- 239	pg.

WAR DIARY
or
INTELLIGENCE SUMMARY.
(Erase heading not required.)

Army Form C. 2118.

Hour, Date, Place	Summary of Events and Information	Remarks and references to Appendices
7-11-14 1 Mile N of YPRES on YPRES-VLAMERTINGHE Rd	YPRES on fire, due to Shell the night before and as far as can be judged enemy firing fire shells; the R.E. and men of N°6 Field ambulance which is close to billets near the end of our drive (hopes) in putting out the fire with the police. The rifle and machine gun fire were dismally heard daily; most of the shells sound as appears to go into YPRES though many fall near the Railway Crossing and the Railway Station on the YPRES-VLAMERTINGE R? about 3/4 mile away. N°6 Field Ambulance kindly sent 2 Medical Officers, 1 N.C.O. & 12 Men to help us during last night, this gave some of our personnel a	PMS

Hour, Date, Place	Summary of Events and Information	Remarks and references to Appendices
7-11-14 cont'd	A much needed night in bed. Capt Loughnan R.A.M.C. passed through the dressing Station today:- Shrapnel wound right arm. Casualties :- 3.0.3	1919.

WAR DIARY
INTELLIGENCE SUMMARY

Army Form C. 2118.

Hour, Date, Place	Summary of Events and Information	Remarks and references to Appendices
8-11-14 1 mile n. of YPRES. on the YPRES-VLAMERTINGHE R^D	Casualties:- 163 No 3693 Pte. Furness Rennie injured from hospital	PM9.

Army Form C. 2118.

WAR DIARY
or
INTELLIGENCE SUMMARY.
(Erase heading not required.)

Hour, Date, Place	Summary of Events and Information	Remarks and references to Appendices
9-11-14 1 mile W of YPRES	The town of YPRES is burning more fiercely than ever this evening. This afternoon the g.t Field Ambulance came staged for a while on the road outside the the Chateau. Last night there were much fewer casualties. The D.A.D.M.S. returned with 2nd Echelon of 2nd Division Staff to POPERINGHE from YPRES. The A.D.M.S. still remains at previous address. Beaver Division still at Farm in road angle just W of HOLLEBEKE R? at ZILLEBEKE Lake. Casualties = 59	1914

Army Form C. 2118.

WAR DIARY
or
INTELLIGENCE SUMMARY.
(Erase heading not required.)

Instructions regarding War Diaries and Intelligence Summaries are contained in F. S. Regs., Part II. and the Staff Manual respectively. Title pages will be prepared in manuscript.

Hour, Date, Place	Summary of Events and Information	Remarks and references to Appendices
10-11-14 1 mile W of YPRES.	Wet weather began. German Shells bursting along road about 200 yards front of Chateau during night, as the French Infantry Came up. Casualties = 60. Lieut. O'Hehir arrived for duty. N° 325 Driver W.H. Clarke A.S.C. } arrived for duty N°/52574 " R Wheeler A.S.C }	[signature]

Army Form C. 2118.

WAR DIARY
or
INTELLIGENCE SUMMARY.
(Erase heading not required.)

Instructions regarding War Diaries and Intelligence Summaries are contained in F.S. Regs., Part II. and the Staff Manual respectively. Title pages will be prepared in manuscript.

Hour, Date, Place	Summary of Events and Information	Remarks and references to Appendices
11-11-14 1 mile NW of YPRES	London Scottish began to come in. One Officer of the London Scottish died during night :- Capt: Ker-Gulland. Deaths while at Chateau Carl now amounted to 60. To Nonne Germans tried to during day Evacuates Casualties 107 No 8729 A/Serjt F. Guy No 10242 Pte J. Snow ⎫ Arrived for duty No 1494 " J. Kilpatrick No 10315 " S.A. Richmond ⎭	KMY

Army Form C. 2118.

WAR DIARY
or
INTELLIGENCE SUMMARY.
(Erase heading not required.)

Instructions regarding War Diaries and Intelligence Summaries are contained in F. S. Regs., Part II, and the Staff Manual respectively. Title pages will be prepared in manuscript.

Hour, Date, Place	Summary of Events and Information	Remarks and references to Appendices
12-11-14 1 Mile N of YPRES	2 Wounded Germans reported by gunners in farm 500 yards away. Sent L/Corpl & 2 men with Medical Offr Capt to bring them in. Casualties 180.	MKQ

WAR DIARY
or
INTELLIGENCE SUMMARY.

(Erase heading not required.)

Army Form C. 2118.

Hour, Date, Place	Summary of Events and Information	Remarks and references to Appendices
13-11-14 1 Mile N of YPRES	Casualties:- 335. No. 10190 Pte. S. Liddiat Transferred to 2 Div. H.Qrs.	1919.

Army Form C. 2118.

WAR DIARY
or
INTELLIGENCE SUMMARY.
(Erase heading not required.)

Hour, Date, Place	Summary of Events and Information	Remarks and references to Appendices
14-11-14 1 mile N of YPRES	Casualties = 135. No 4401 Corpl. Barker arrived for duty	

Army Form C. 2118.

WAR DIARY
or
INTELLIGENCE SUMMARY.
(Erase heading not required.)

Instructions regarding War Diaries and Intelligence Summaries are contained in F.S. Regs., Part II. and the Staff Manual respectively. Title pages will be prepared in manuscript.

Hour, Date, Place	Summary of Events and Information	Remarks and references to Appendices
15-11-14 1 mile N of YPRES.	Casualties - 108	MR9.

WAR DIARY
or
INTELLIGENCE SUMMARY.

(Erase heading not required.)

Army Form C. 2118.

Hour, Date, Place	Summary of Events and Information	Remarks and references to Appendices
16-11-14	Deaths up-to-date in Cholera. 73. Orders received last night that 2nd Division are to be relieved to-night at the latest. They were relieved during evening. Sick List began to come in during evening. No of Canadian = 96.	DMG

Copy

Operation Orders by Col M P Holt
A.D.M.S. 2nd Division   D.S.O.

M.22.   17th Novr. 1-0 pm.

1. Bearer Division will remain with Lord Cavan's Brigade at ZILLEBEKE.

2. Bearer Division 5 F.A. will remain at White Horse Cottage (Dressing Station) at K.2½ on YPRES–ZONNEBEKE Road with additional three Ambulance Wagons from No.6 F.A.

3. Bt. Div 6 F.A. will rejoin headquarters of Unit to-day at 1K W of Y– POPERINGHE Road, less three Ambulance Wagons lent to Bd Div 5 F.A.

4. In absence of A.D.M.S. O.C. Bd Div 5 F.A. will make all arrangements for evacuation of Sick Wounded of 5th Bde. an R.A. Btries will wire daily to A.D.M.S. for Motor Ambulances required not later than 1-0 pm Daily 5th Bde Headqrs are at

From N of R3 on YPRES-MENIN Road,
H'qrs of II Div at POPERINGHE
43 Rue L'HOPITAL
Signal Station at CHATEAU-POTIJZE

(Sd) M.P. Holt D.S.O.
Colonel ADMS

WAR DIARY
or
INTELLIGENCE SUMMARY.

(Erase heading not required.)

Army Form C. 2118.

Hour, Date, Place	Summary of Events and Information	Remarks and references to Appendices
17-11-14	No 4 Canadian Is7. No T/32254 Driver Wheeler (ASC) transferred to 6th FA Divn	1919

Copy.

R.A.M.C. Operation Orders.

By Col. M.P. Holt. A.D.M.S. 2nd Division

8.45 pm 18-11-14

① No 6 F. Amb. less 3 Ambulance wagons, will proceed tomorrow morning to occupy Billets in CAESTRE

② No 5 F. Amb., less Bearer Division will proceed tomorrow morning to occupy Billets in BAILLEUL

③ No 4 F. Amb. Tent Division will occupy present Dressing Station until instructions received to proceed with Bearer Division to Billets in METEREN. Instructions re this movement will be issued by Lord Cavan.

Bearer division No 4 F.A. will act under instructions from Lord Cavan.

④ Bearer Division No 5 F Ambulance will join the Tent Division at BAILLEUL when so directed by Col Westmacott

ROUTE. The route taken to be via RENINGHELST and WESTOUTRE as the DICKEBUSCH — BAILLEUL road is subject to shell fire

Army Form C. 2118.

WAR DIARY
or
INTELLIGENCE SUMMARY.
(Erase heading not required.)

Instructions regarding War Diaries and Intelligence Summaries are contained in F. S. Regs., Part II. and the Staff Manual respectively. Title pages will be prepared in manuscript.

Hour, Date, Place	Summary of Events and Information	Remarks and references to Appendices
18-11-14	N° of Casualties :- 61.	Jno

Army Form C. 2118.

WAR DIARY
or
INTELLIGENCE SUMMARY.
(Erase heading not required.)

Hour, Date, Place	Summary of Events and Information	Remarks and references to Appendices
19-11-14 1 Mile N of YPRES.	Put under Lord Cavan's orders, by order of A.D.M.S. During evening orders came from 4th Inf Brigade saying that we were to march independently next day to METEREN, and not to arrive before 3 p.m. The Cavan Division to proceed with the Brigade. N° of Casualties :- 21	PAG

WAR DIARY
or
INTELLIGENCE SUMMARY.

(Erase heading not required.)

Army Form C. 2118.

Hour, Date, Place	Summary of Events and Information	Remarks and references to Appendices
20-11-14	Left Chateau, 1 mile N of YPRES at 8 a.m. Via VLAMERTINGHE — DUDERDON — RENING — HELST — WESTOUTRE to METEREN. Arrived 3-10 p.m.	

Army Form C. 2118.

WAR DIARY
or
INTELLIGENCE SUMMARY.
(Erase heading not required.)

Instructions regarding War Diaries and Intelligence Summaries are contained in F. S. Regs., Part II. and the Staff Manual respectively. Title pages will be prepared in manuscript.

Hour, Date, Place	Summary of Events and Information	Remarks and references to Appendices
21–11–14 METEREN	Billets in Church Square. Officers billeted in Curé's House. Two hospital wards in two houses along side the streets above the other, and in this building are Cook House, Officers' & N.C.O. Room. Cooking was also done in a yard at the back of Cook House. Hospital latrines trenches along side of road). In small grass enclosure. Officers' mess in Farm house at corner of Street. W of Grass enclosure. The men were accommodated in Barns in the Farm.	PRG

Army Form C. 2118.

WAR DIARY
or
INTELLIGENCE SUMMARY.
(Erase heading not required.)

Instructions regarding War Diaries and Intelligence Summaries are contained in F.S. Regs., Part II. and the Staff Manual respectively. Title pages will be prepared in manuscript.

Hour, Date, Place	Summary of Events and Information	Remarks and references to Appendices
21—11—14 Cont'd	A.S.C. personnel in a barn by themselves. Officers mess Latrines in garden behind hospital ward. The Peru'n Division had to make arrangements at a point near railway station for the evacuation of wounded near to YPRES for the evacuation of wounded & 7th Field Ambulance were thus delayed. The Bearer Division arrived under Capt. Boyce & Leut. McCullagh from their advanced dressing station near ZILLEBEKE at 3 (p.m.) They left behind Lieut. Wilson to collect y wounded from 7th Field Ambulance, 3 of these he handed over to French Hospital at RENINGHELST. Leut. Wilson arrived at 6 p.m. No of Sick = 34	PAY.

WAR DIARY or INTELLIGENCE SUMMARY.

(Erase heading not required.)

Army Form C. 2118.

Hour, Date, Place	Summary of Events and Information	Remarks and references to Appendices
22-11-14 METEREN	Church Service in barn at 5.30 pm. Leave granted to Officers in two periods of five days; The first period was extended to 7 days except Capt. Blackwell to 6 days N° 4 Sick = 50 Capt. Blackwell Capt. Boyd } Went for leave. Lieut. Bryan Lieut. Lowe Lieut. Qrmr. Jones.	1919

WAR DIARY or INTELLIGENCE SUMMARY

Army Form C. 2118.

Hour, Date, Place	Summary of Events and Information	Remarks and references to Appendices
23-11-14 METEREN	2 N.C.O. recommended for period of leave of 5 days. S/Sergt. Fries try regimt. goes on 2nd period. S/Sergt. Todd on 1st. Father Bradley went to 18th Field Ambulance for duty. Lower unit to be used as Medical Inspection Room except in case of overflow. Lieut. McCullagh sent on leave. S/Sergt. Todd went on leave. N° of sick = 16.	AMQ

Army Form C. 2118.

WAR DIARY
or
INTELLIGENCE SUMMARY.
(Erase heading not required.)

Instructions regarding War Diaries and Intelligence Summaries are contained in F. S. Regs., Part II. and the Staff Manual respectively. Title pages will be prepared in manuscript.

Hour, Date, Place	Summary of Events and Information	Remarks and references to Appendices
24-11-14 METEREN	Visit from A.D.M.S 10 of Sick = 19	AMQ

Army Form C. 2118.

WAR DIARY
or
INTELLIGENCE SUMMARY.
(Erase heading not required.)

Instructions regarding War Diaries and Intelligence Summaries are contained in F. S. Regs., Part II. and the Staff Manual respectively. Title pages will be prepared in manuscript.

Hour, Date, Place	Summary of Events and Information	Remarks and references to Appendices
25-11-14 METEREN	Visit to clerks Tent Regt. Lord Hampden commanding Instructed them on the art of execution N° of Sick = 11	PMO

Army Form C. 2118.

WAR DIARY
or
INTELLIGENCE SUMMARY
(Erase heading not required.)

Instructions regarding War Diaries and Intelligence Summaries are contained in F. S. Regs., Part II. and the Staff Manual respectively. Title pages will be prepared in manuscript.

Hour, Date, Place	Summary of Events and Information	Remarks and references to Appendices
26-11-14 METEREN	N° of Sick = 9	PPQ

Army Form C. 2118.

WAR DIARY
or
INTELLIGENCE SUMMARY.
(Erase heading not required.)

Hour, Date, Place	Summary of Events and Information	Remarks and references to Appendices
29-11-16 METEREN	Colonel Feilding, Coldstream Guards acting Brigadier made his inspection of Brigade Area this morning. I accompanied him. Brigadier General Lord Cavan returned in evening. Inspection by A.D.M.S in afternoon. There has been a certain amount of suffering among men of Brigade lately due to the cold, causing painful swollen feet; one or two of these cases have a definite cause, for instance AORTIC disease, but most of them are entirely due to cold especially tight fitting puttees &c The total of these cases on 21 up to 16. date, of there 8 have been returned to duty, 15 evacuated to Clearing Hospital, in Hazebrouck & 8 are still under	PMS F.C.

Army Form C. 2118.

WAR DIARY
or
INTELLIGENCE SUMMARY
(Erase heading not required.)

Instructions regarding War Diaries and Intelligence Summaries are contained in F.S. Regs., Part II. and the Staff Manual respectively. Title pages will be prepared in manuscript.

Hour, Date, Place	Summary of Events and Information	Remarks and references to Appendices
27-11-18 METEREN	Treatment in Divisional Station No. of Sick = 14 No. 8191 Pte. Stanfield to Hospital	PMG

Army Form C. 2118.

WAR DIARY
or
INTELLIGENCE SUMMARY.
(Erase heading not required.)

Hour, Date, Place	Summary of Events and Information	Remarks and references to Appendices
28-11-14 METEREN	Staff/Capt Jones went for 5 days leave. N° of Sick - 20 N° 23895 Driver Mathews A.S.C. to Hospital sick Capt. Blackwell returned from leave Capt. P.A. Rhys-Jones ⎫ Lieut H.D. Martin ⎬ went on leave. Lieut O. Wilson ⎭	pmg

Army Form C. 2118.

WAR DIARY
or
INTELLIGENCE SUMMARY.
(Erase heading not required.)

Instructions regarding War Diaries and Intelligence Summaries are contained in F.S. Regs., Part II. and the Staff Manual respectively. Title pages will be prepared in manuscript.

Hour, Date, Place	Summary of Events and Information	Remarks and references to Appendices
29-11-14 METEREN	Nov Sect=12 Capt. Boyce R.A.M.C. returned from leave. Lieut. Dyas R.A.M.C. returned from leave. Lieut. Lovell R.A.M.C. returned from leave.	PMO

Army Form C. 2118.

WAR DIARY
or
INTELLIGENCE SUMMARY.
(Erase heading not required.)

Instructions regarding War Diaries and Intelligence Summaries are contained in F.S. Regs., Part II. and the Staff Manual respectively. Title pages will be prepared in manuscript.

Hour, Date, Place	Summary of Events and Information	Remarks and references to Appendices
30.11.14 METEREN	Lieut MacDonald left to report to D.D.M.S. 2HQ STONER for duty N° of Sick = 14	DMQ

5th Field Ambulance

Vol V

121/38/72
Dec 1914

Army Form C. 2118.

WAR DIARY
or
INTELLIGENCE SUMMARY.
(Erase heading not required.)

Hour, Date, Place	Summary of Events and Information	Remarks and references to Appendices
Dec 1st METEREN	Lieut McCullagh returned from leave. No of sick 19	PM9

WAR DIARY
or
INTELLIGENCE SUMMARY

(*Erase heading not required.*)

Army Form C. 2118.

Instructions regarding War Diaries and Intelligence Summaries are contained in F.S. Regs., Part II and the Staff Manual respectively. Title pages will be prepared in manuscript.

Hour, Date, Place	Summary of Events and Information	Remarks and references to Appendices
2nd December/14 METEREN	W⁰ of Sick 35	(M9)

Copy 2/12/14

Following wire from 2nd Div begins

"His Majesty the King will pass through area of 1st Corps today 2nd Dec AAA Troops will not be paraded but all Troops along the road must be cautioned to halt when His Majesty passes and to salute message ends.

Probable time of passing through METEREN between 3.30 to 5 pm

Army Form C. 2118.

WAR DIARY
or
INTELLIGENCE SUMMARY.
(Erase heading not required.)

Instructions regarding War Diaries and Intelligence Summaries are contained in F. S. Regs., Part II. and the Staff Manual respectively. Title pages will be prepared in manuscript.

Hour, Date, Place	Summary of Events and Information	Remarks and references to Appendices
3rd December/14 METEREN	Paraded at 10.30 am for inspection by His Majesty the King. His Majesty inspected the unit at 12.15 pm. All available Officers, N.C.Officers, men were present. No. of Sheet 5.	

Army Form C. 2118.

WAR DIARY
or
INTELLIGENCE SUMMARY.
(Erase heading not required.)

Instructions regarding War Diaries and Intelligence Summaries are contained in F.S. Regs., Part II and the Staff Manual respectively. Title pages will be prepared in manuscript.

Hour, Date, Place	Summary of Events and Information	Remarks and references to Appendices
4th December/14 METEREN	S/Sergt Pepper went on leave Sergt Friman (A.S.C) went on leave Sergt Mann went on leave Order recd for retirement of leave to Officers until Sunday night the 6th. Order from Brigade Major for 4th Brigade to hold themselves in readiness to move from the 5th at 8 am to 6th 8 am No of Sick - 16	[signature]

Army Form C. 2118.

WAR DIARY
or
INTELLIGENCE SUMMARY.
(Erase heading not required.)

Instructions regarding War Diaries and Intelligence Summaries are contained in F. S. Regs., Part II and the Staff Manual respectively. Title pages will be prepared in manuscript.

Hour, Date, Place	Summary of Events and Information	Remarks and references to Appendices
December 5th 1914 METEREN	N° of sick – 26	OK9

Army Form C. 2118.

WAR DIARY
or
INTELLIGENCE SUMMARY.
(Erase heading not required.)

Instructions regarding War Diaries and Intelligence Summaries are contained in F. S. Regs., Part II and the Staff Manual respectively. Title pages will be prepared in manuscript.

Hour, Date, Place	Summary of Events and Information	Remarks and references to Appendices
December 6th 1914 METEREN	Capt. P.O. Lloyd-Jones returned from leave. No. of sick 8	PRO

Army Form C. 2118.

WAR DIARY
or
INTELLIGENCE SUMMARY.
(Erase heading not required.)

Instructions regarding War Diaries and Intelligence Summaries are contained in F. S. Regs., Part II and the Staff Manual respectively. Title pages will be prepared in manuscript.

Hour, Date, Place	Summary of Events and Information	Remarks and references to Appendices
December 9th 1917 METEREN	S/Sgt Jones returned from leave. No of rank 10	17719.

WAR DIARY
or
INTELLIGENCE SUMMARY.
(Erase heading not required.)

Army Form C. 2118.

Hour, Date, Place	Summary of Events and Information	Remarks and references to Appendices
December 8th 1914 METEREN	Serjt Pepper ⎱ Sergt Moon ⎱ Returns from leave Serjt Freeman ⎰ No. of Sick. 8. Recommendations through ADMS. Capt. J.S. Blackwell ⎱ mention in dispatches Capt. W.W. Boyce ⎰ Lieut. McK. McCullagh - for Mount. S-Sgt. Ripper ⎱ Sgt. Hulliver ⎱ mention in dispatches Pte. Rogers ⎰ Pte. Marshall ⎱ for award Pte. Lucas ⎰	OM9 OM9

Army Form C. 2118.

WAR DIARY
or
INTELLIGENCE SUMMARY.
(Erase heading not required.)

Instructions regarding War Diaries and Intelligence Summaries are contained in F. S. Regs., Part II. and the Staff Manual respectively. Title pages will be prepared in manuscript.

Hour, Date, Place	Summary of Events and Information	Remarks and references to Appendices
Dec 9th 1914 METEREN	Visit from ADMS 2nd Division. No of sick - 9.	PAQ.

Army Form C. 2118.

WAR DIARY
or
INTELLIGENCE SUMMARY.

(Erase heading not required.)

Instructions regarding War Diaries and Intelligence Summaries are contained in F.S. Regs., Part II and the Staff Manual respectively. Title pages will be prepared in manuscript.

Hour, Date, Place	Summary of Events and Information	Remarks and references to Appendices
December 10th/14 METEREN	Private 50449 Jones J. transferred to 1st Siege Artillery Brigade No. of sick = 5	OK4

WAR DIARY
or
INTELLIGENCE SUMMARY.
(Erase heading not required.)

Army Form C. 2118.

Hour, Date, Place	Summary of Events and Information	Remarks and references to Appendices
December 11th 1914 METEREN	4 (Guards) Brigade under orders to move at short notice between 8 am 11th to 8 am 12th. No of Iuk ?	Only

Army Form C. 2118.

WAR DIARY
or
INTELLIGENCE SUMMARY.
(Erase heading not required.)

Instructions regarding War Diaries and Intelligence Summaries are contained in F.S. Regs., Part II. and the Staff Manual respectively. Title pages will be prepared in manuscript.

Hour, Date, Place	Summary of Events and Information	Remarks and references to Appendices
Dec 12th/14 METEREN	Lieut H.M. Cooke arrived for duty. Nov casualty stamps received and all one destroyed. N.T.R. Sick 3.	ORG

Army Form C. 2118.

WAR DIARY
or
INTELLIGENCE SUMMARY.
(Erase heading not required.)

Instructions regarding War Diaries and Intelligence Summaries are contained in F.S. Regs., Part II. and the Staff Manual respectively. Title pages will be prepared in manuscript.

Hour, Date, Place	Summary of Events and Information	Remarks and references to Appendices
December 13th 1914 METEREN	Orders received to be ready to move after 9am the 14th at 2 hours notice. N° of Sick = 4	CKJ

Copy.   13/12/14

2nd Div Wires :- All troops in your area will be ready to move at two hours notice from 9 am tomorrow AAA Baggage wagons to be packed AAA Arrangements are to be made for the return of surplus gifts to store at Hazebrouck in accordance with instructions which will be issued AAA Acknowledge.

4th Guards Brigade

Army Form C. 2118.

WAR DIARY
or
INTELLIGENCE SUMMARY.
(Erase heading not required.)

Instructions regarding War Diaries and Intelligence Summaries are contained in F.S. Regs., Part II and the Staff Manual respectively. Title pages will be prepared in manuscript.

Hour, Date, Place	Summary of Events and Information	Remarks and references to Appendices
December 14th 1914 METEREN	Still under orders to move at 2 hours notice. No. of Sick = 9.	OR4/

WAR DIARY
or
INTELLIGENCE SUMMARY.
(Erase heading not required.)

Army Form C. 2118.

Hour, Date, Place	Summary of Events and Information	Remarks and references to Appendices
December 15th/14 METEREN	No. 5973 Pte Busby Ranle Transferred to 2nd Green Esto No. 3615 " Costello W. " do to 1st Irish " No. 1490 " Abrahams S " do " 2nd Monar Reft No. 4689 " Myers S " do " 2nd H.R.J. No. 6290 " Fletcher R " do " 2nd J.L.J. No. 3693 " Furness W " do " 11th Coy R.E. (No. of Sick - 8) Instructed in their duties.	DRW

Army Form C. 2118.

WAR DIARY
or
INTELLIGENCE SUMMARY
(Erase heading not required.)

Instructions regarding War Diaries and Intelligence Summaries are contained in F.S. Regs., Part II. and the Staff Manual respectively. Title pages will be prepared in manuscript.

Hour, Date, Place	Summary of Events and Information	Remarks and references to Appendices
December 16th 1914 METEREN	No. of Sick 1 - 6	PM9

Copy 15/12/14

2nd Divn Wires

The first Corps will be in Army reserve tomorrow as to-day AAA

2nd Division will be in readiness to move at two hours notice.

Please acknowledge

4th Guards Brigade

Army Form C. 2118.

WAR DIARY
or
INTELLIGENCE SUMMARY.

(*Erase heading not required.*)

Instructions regarding War Diaries and Intelligence Summaries are contained in F. S. Regs., Part II and the Staff Manual respectively. Title pages will be prepared in manuscript.

Hour, Date, Place	Summary of Events and Information	Remarks and references to Appendices
Dec 17th/14 METEREN	No of Sick - 4	OM9

Army Form C. 2118.

WAR DIARY
or
INTELLIGENCE SUMMARY.
(Erase heading not required.)

Instructions regarding War Diaries and Intelligence Summaries are contained in F. S. Regs., Part II. and the Staff Manual respectively. Title pages will be prepared in manuscript.

Hour, Date, Place	Summary of Events and Information	Remarks and references to Appendices
December 15th/14 METEREN	No. of Sick = 4	ORY

Army Form C. 2118.

WAR DIARY
or
INTELLIGENCE SUMMARY.
(Erase heading not required.)

Instructions regarding War Diaries and Intelligence Summaries are contained in F.S. Regs., Part II and the Staff Manual respectively. Title pages will be prepared in manuscript.

Hour, Date, Place	Summary of Events and Information	Remarks and references to Appendices
December 19th 1914 METEREN	No 8989 Pte McArdle J Transferred to Base Hospt. No of Sick = 5.	DRg

WAR DIARY
or
INTELLIGENCE SUMMARY.
(Erase heading not required.)

Army Form C. 2118.

Hour, Date, Place	Summary of Events and Information	Remarks and references to Appendices
December 24th/14 METEREN	N° 19711 Corpt Hitchins S.L. Rawls " 6386 Pinto Price w/s " 18764 " Kenion H " 910 " Mills A " 7916 " King S " 4048 " Quinn & Sgt " 733 " Rogers & Sgt " 14215 " Fraser G " 18459 " Daniels V " 9327 " Osborn R.A. N.H Sick - 2	Award for Mutg OK y

WAR DIARY or INTELLIGENCE SUMMARY

Army Form C. 2118.

(Erase heading not required.)

Hour, Date, Place	Summary of Events and Information	Remarks and references to Appendices
December 21st/14 METEREN	4th (Guards) Brigade under one hour notice to move. 1st & 2nd Field Ambulance and 11th Coy R.E. also under 2 hours notice to move. Promotions No. 9449 Corpl Suant promoted Sergt } " 6386 Private Price " to Corpl } 12.12.14 Visit from D.D.M.S. 1st Army Corps and A.D.M.S. 2nd Division No. of Sick 2	PKg /

Copy 21st/12/14

Second division will be ready
to move at 7 am tomorrow
AAA Orders follow

4th Bde

"Copy   21ᵒⁿ/12/14

Reference to wire from 2nd
Division ordering 4th (Guards)
Brigade & 41" F A Brigade to
be ready to move at one hour's
notice, please note that in case
they move off 11th Field Coy &
4th Field Ambulance will continue
to hold themselves in readiness
to move off at two hours notice.

Army Form C. 2118.

WAR DIARY
or
INTELLIGENCE SUMMARY.

(Erase heading not required.)

Hour, Date, Place	Summary of Events and Information	Remarks and references to Appendices
December 22nd METEREN	Left METEREN at 9 a.m. and arrived at BETHUNE at 7.30 p.m. Billetted in Rue De GENDARMERIE for one night in a Stables, left & 2 horses. No. of Sick = Nil. Marched through OUTERSTEEN, VIEUX BERQUIN, NEUVE BERQUIN, MERVILLE & LOCON to BETHUNE.	OOK1/

Army Form C. 2118.

WAR DIARY
or
INTELLIGENCE SUMMARY.
(Erase heading not required.)

Instructions regarding War Diaries and Intelligence Summaries are contained in F. S. Regs., Part II and the Staff Manual respectively. Title pages will be prepared in manuscript.

Hour, Date, Place	Summary of Events and Information	Remarks and references to Appendices
December 23rd BETHUNE	Lieut B.A. Murphy arrived for duty. Took over a portion of the Duties of Field Ambulance (Indian Army). Dispositions made as follows: I Evacuation wing to enter by gate in RUE-ST-PRY and travels through gate in Square at lower end of RUE-DU-JEU-DE-PAUME. II Small wing hut offside to soldiers quarters used as office for taking names of cases as they pass in wagon. III Casualty tram fitted for dressing and examination of cases to right of main door.	M.O.

WAR DIARY
INTELLIGENCE SUMMARY.
(Erase heading not required.)

Army Form C. 2118.

Hour, Date, Place	Summary of Events and Information	Remarks and references to Appendices
December 25th BETHUNE	1st visited LOCON to meet A.D.M.S and officers commanding 5th & 6th Field Ambulances. Decided that 4th Field Ambulance should so marshal the area of the 4th (Guards) Infantry Brigade as the G.O.C 4th Brigade has asked for them. For the present dressing station to remain in BETHUNE. Took over from 5th Field Ambulance 1. Estaminet 2. Private House 3. Farm on road turning off from right to prevent road in LOCON. These buildings to be retained so long as necessary with a view to moving forward later.	OK/

45

WAR DIARY
or
INTELLIGENCE SUMMARY.
(Erase heading not required.)

Army Form C. 2118.

Hour, Date, Place	Summary of Events and Information	Remarks and references to Appendices
Dec 23rd Cont^d BETHUNE	IV Sisters kept repairs and brought huts into use. V Two wards with room for 75 cases in each, with photo latrines + pantry attached to each, one dressing room formed for each ward VI Acting Medical Officers room VII Burial Case admitted to reserve line of huts. Telware rooms and fresh underclothes VIII Latrines and incinerators made to N.A. Dressing Station in garden flat. and incinerators in centre of yard N. of Dressing Station	PMQ.

WAR DIARY
or
INTELLIGENCE SUMMARY.
(Erase heading not required.)

Army Form C. 2118.

Hour, Date, Place.	Summary of Events and Information	Remarks and references to Appendices
December 28th/14 BETHUNE (contd)	IX An old building at NE corner of Square take over and dispositions made as follows :- A Tool house on ground floor for which a store was requisitioned in the Town B Offices of Mr. Brenton Motors Store C Pack Store also on ground floor D Our Pack Store, held for use in shop Sect 150. Capacity of machines Shop Sect 150. Capacity of machines in old building 130. Total 280 Roof - Sect 2	OKg.

Copy

O.C. N° 4 Field Ambulance

Open advanced Dressing Station on road immediately West of L in RUE DE L'EPINETTE (Square P9). Your Bearer Sub-Division will be stationed site selected by Capt. Boyce in Square P7. Tent Division will remain at Civil & Military Hospital. Attach Liaison Officer 4th (Guards) Brigade. Take up this disposition daylight tomorrow.

Sgd. F.S. Irvine
Major R.A.M.C.
D.A.D.M.S. 2 Div.

24/1/14

Copy

Please meet A.D.M.S. 2nd Division at 9.30 am to-morrow (25-12-14) at MEERUT Division Headquarters LOCON.

H.Q. 2 Div
24-12-14

(Sgd) JS Irvine
Major RAMC
DADMS

Army Form C. 2118.

WAR DIARY
or
INTELLIGENCE SUMMARY.
(Erase heading not required.)

Instructions regarding War Diaries and Intelligence Summaries are contained in F. S. Regs., Part II. and the Staff Manual respectively. Title pages will be prepared in manuscript.

Hour, Date, Place	Summary of Events and Information	Remarks and references to Appendices
Cont.d 25/10/14 BETHUNE	As the dressing station in BETHUNE is in the 1st Division Area decided to be taken over from them stopped already they were off No. of Sick = 26 Took over (Clearing) thoroughly three removed old building & Scruffies tins out into Creek this enabling me to evacuate beds up to 3TD if necessary.	DMS.

Army Form C. 2118.

WAR DIARY
or
INTELLIGENCE SUMMARY.
(Erase heading not required.)

Instructions regarding War Diaries and Intelligence Summaries are contained in F.S. Regs., Part II and the Staff Manual respectively. Title pages will be prepared in manuscript.

Hour, Date, Place	Summary of Events and Information	Remarks and references to Appendices
December 26th/14 BETHUNE	Inspected Burial Sub Division (formed of Burial Sub-Division of C and ½ Burial Sub-Division of B section under Capt Boyce) which had arrived there at daybreak the day before. Lieut M'Cullagh and ― had broken down with flu. Chaplins Henry arrived during the day. Disposition of Burial Sub Division:— I. RHQ at a point about 300 yards to the East of LE-TOURET in farm house on left of road, two minutes walk from Regale Headquarters. II Advanced dressing station in house on left of road at cross roads, about 3/4 of a mile E from the	RHQ. RHQ

Gillet

No. 4 Field Ambulance.

Capacity -- Officers -- 5
             Other Ranks - 250

	Officers		Other Ranks	
	Sick	Wnded	Sick	Wnded
No. in occupation	—	1	40	117
Lying	—	1	2	6
Sitting	—	—	11	8
Walking	—	—	3	—
Unfit to move	—	—	—	3
Not for evacuation	—	—	24	—

26/12/14
7.45 a.m.

P A Lloyd Jones
Capt. R.A.M.C.
O.C. 4th. Field Amb⁄

D.D.M.S.
  1st Army Corps.

1st Field Ambulance

Capacity – Officers – 3
Other ranks – 250

	Officers		Other Ranks	
	Sick	Wounded	Sick	Wounded
Remaining			41	10
Dying			3	–
Sitting			28	8
Walking			5	–
Unfit to move			–	2
Not for evacuation			3	–

P.A. H[...]
Lt Col
1st Field Amb.

6/5/1916

No 4 Field Ambulance

Capacity: Officers = 3
Other Ranks = 250

	Officers		Other Ranks	
	Sick	Wnd	Sick	Wnd
NE in Occupation	2	2	51	16
Lying			3	3
Sitting			34	12
Walking			12	-
Unfit to move			-	41
Fit for evacuation	2	2	9	-

5.45 p.m.
26.12.14

O.E. Dyas
A.R.M.C.
to Capt Kane
OC 4 Fd Amb.

Army Form C. 2118.

WAR DIARY
or
INTELLIGENCE SUMMARY.
(Erase heading not required.)

Instructions regarding War Diaries and Intelligence Summaries are contained in F. S. Regs., Part II. and the Staff Manual respectively. Title pages will be prepared in manuscript.

Hour, Date, Place	Summary of Events and Information	Remarks and references to Appendices
Dec 26th/14 Cont'd BETHUNE	III Collecting point 2 men established by side of road at place where wounded are brought by regimental stretcher bearers, one of these men to bring back a message to Advanced dressing station when casualties arrive there. This is about 400 yards from the trenches Medical Officers of Regiments in front trenches will of the advanced dressing station Visited G.O.C. 11th Infantry Brigade and discussed line of evacuation to him He said he was satisfied Gave him dispositions in writing	PRO

Army Form C. 2118.

WAR DIARY
or
INTELLIGENCE SUMMARY.
(Erase heading not required.)

Hour, Date, Place	Summary of Events and Information	Remarks and references to Appendices
December 27th/14 BETHUNE	Capt. Blackwell notified me that he has taken over details from the Indian Hospital. Majors Hill & Kerr wish to LOCON for my new leave asking for their motors. I am to be kept at Ad Dressing Station at the dressing station at BETHUNE. II Whenever a loaded motor Ambulance arrives at the dressing station and empty one must be sent immediately to the advanced dressing station. III For the present all sick and lightly wounded will be transported in the Stores wagons, except to fill up wagons otherwise already containing lying down cases, but as far as possible the sick & Ambulance	PAC 9

Field Ambulance

Capacity – Officers 6.
Other Ranks 250

	Officers		Other Ranks	
	Sick	Wnd	Sick	Wnd
Now in occupation	1	3	68	22
Lying	–	1	3	10
Sitting	–	–	44	9
Walking	–	–	4	9
Unfit to move	–	–	–	–
Not for evacuation	1	2	17	1

27/12/17
8 a.m.

G E Dyas L/Cpl RAMC
for Capt R Hine
O.C. 4th Fd Amb

D.D.M.S.
1st Army Corps.

No. 4 Field Ambulance

Capacity - Officers 6
             Other Ranks 220

	Officers		Other Ranks	
	Sick	Wnd	Sick	Wnd
In occupation	1	1	66	11
Lying			—	—
Sitting			44	11
Walking			3	—
Unfit to move			—	—
Fit for evacuation	1	1	16	—

24/8/14
10.30 a.m.

P A L[?] Jones
Capt RAMC
OC 4 Fd Amb

ADMS
1st Army Corps.

No 4 Field Ambulance

Capacity:- Officers 8
Others Ranks 230

	Officers		Other Ranks	
	Sick	Wnd	Sick	Wnd
In occupation	1	1	67	5
Lying			—	1
Sitting			22	2
Walking			—	—
Unfit to move				
Fit for evacuation	1	1	45	2

P.A. Lloyd Jones.
Capt RAMC
O.C. 4 Fd Amb.

1 ft./500
5.30 p.m.

D.A.D.M.S
1st Army Corps

WAR DIARY
or
INTELLIGENCE SUMMARY.
(Erase heading not required.)

Army Form C. 2118.

Instructions regarding War Diaries and Intelligence Summaries are contained in F.S. Regs., Part II and the Staff Manual respectively. Title pages will be prepared in manuscript.

Hour, Date, Place	Summary of Events and Information	Remarks and references to Appendices
December 27/14 Cont. BETHUNE	Dugout will only be used for seriously wounded. Permission obtained from M LE DIRECTEUR to use operating theatre in hospital. Arrangements placed in the hands of Capt. Smith (C.S.) Capt McKerron to be N.C.O in charge of these arrangements. After treatment of cases to be conducted in the French surgical wards. <u>Evacuation</u> Ambulance trains realised at 6 a.m 12 noon and 6 p.m. to D.D.M.S. 1st Army Corps. Every assistance given by M. LE Maire and M LE DIRECTEUR	O.R.g.

Army Form C. 2118.

WAR DIARY
or
INTELLIGENCE SUMMARY.
(Erase heading not required.)

Instructions regarding War Diaries and Intelligence Summaries are contained in F. S. Regs., Part II and the Staff Manual respectively. Title pages will be prepared in manuscript.

Hour, Date, Place	Summary of Events and Information	Remarks and references to Appendices
December 29/14 Con'd BETHUNE	Officers Dressing Station established at No 4 Rue. St. Pry. 5 Beds provided, also nursing orderlies & 1 G.D.O. noted there. Had returned by requisition from town a cheval trine obtained as overflow with 3 beds in Square N of Main Dressing Station. Officers brought to Main Dressing Station for inspection and treatment before being taken to their homes. Duties of Officers:- I — Bearer Sub Division — A Officer 1/c Capt Pryce B — Tiernan Officer at 1st Infantry Brigade E Officer Lieut Cooke (CS)	PMJ

Army Form C. 2118.

WAR DIARY
or
INTELLIGENCE SUMMARY.
(Erase heading not required.)

Hour, Date, Place	Summary of Events and Information	Remarks and references to Appendices
December 29th/14 Camp — BETHUNE	I. Officer working with Medical Officer i/c of Regiment. Lieut. McGinley (SR) Lieut. Dyas	(PKg)
	II. Major Gatun at LACON	
	III. Draining Station	(PKg)
	A. Officer Commands Capt Blackwell	
	B. In charge of Officer for anti-tetanus when not on guard Lieut Bond (CS)	
	C. Officers doing duty in wards:—	
	Lieut Molto	
	Lieut Murphy	
	Lieut Miller	
	Quartermaster Lieut Morton	
	11° N° Cavalry 5th Lieut. Wither arrive for duty	

WAR DIARY
or
INTELLIGENCE SUMMARY.
(Erase heading not required.)

Army Form C. 2118.

Hour, Date, Place	Summary of Events and Information	Remarks and references to Appendices
December 28th/14 BETHUNE	Appointments: No 17974 Cpt Moon F. to be Lance 12244 Pte Leonie J.B. } A/Sgts. 8589 " Farrimore H.J. No 12268 Pte McKernon F. } 255 " Topham J. 7266 " McNeill J. to be 9063 " Newitt G.N. 17043 " Walker N.A. a/cpls 3156 " Davis T. 2571 " Nutt J. 3195 " Martin E. 3158 " Steele R. No 4 Sick 50 Lieut Willis proceeded to 6th F.A. Amb. for duty Sgt Hellman to be Sups. dep. I/c Stores.	PMG

No. 11 Field Ambulance

Capacity — Officers — 25
            Other Ranks 280

	Officers		Other Rks.	
	Sick	Wnd.	Sick	Wnd.
S.I. Occupation	1	1	49	14
Lying	—	—	—	3
Sitting	—	—	—	8
Walking	—	—	—	—
Unfit to move	—	—	—	—
Fit for evacuation	1	1	49	3

28/12/17
7.30 a.m.

P.A.W.
Capt. R.A.M.C.
O.C. 11th Field Ambulance

Copy to
1st Army Corps

No 4 Field Ambulance

Capacity :- Officers 8
Other Ranks 280.

	Officers		Other Ranks	
	Sick	Wnd	Sick	Wounded
In occupation	1	1	50	14
Lying			—	5
Sitting			5	6
Walking			—	—
Unfit to move			—	—
Not for evacuation	1	1	45	3

P. A. Lloyd Jones
Capt. RAMC
OC 4th Fd Amb

28/12/14.
11.30 a.m.

ADMS.
1st Army Corps.

No 4 Field Ambulance

Capacity:- Officers 8
Other Ranks 280

	Officers		Other Ranks	
	Sick	Wnd	Sick	Wnd
In occupation	2	1	88	14
Lying			-	5
Sitting			6	6
Walking			-	-
Unfits to move			-	1
Not for evacuation	2	1	82	2

28/12/14

P. A. Lloyd Jones
Capt RAMC
OC 4 Fd Amb

5. Cop —
ADMS
1st Army Corps

Army Form C. 2118.

WAR DIARY
or
INTELLIGENCE SUMMARY.
(Erase heading not required.)

Hour, Date, Place	Summary of Events and Information	Remarks and references to Appendices

December 29/14
BETHUNE
	Treatment for Swollen Painful feet caused by damp & cold in the trenches.
	
	§ Points
	<u>I</u>. No treatment
	<u>II</u>. General treatment only
	<u>III</u>. Massage & paint stan.
	    to
	    (a) ~~continuity~~ Intermittent pmg.
	    (b) Onophnity
	<u>IV</u>. Calcium Lactate –
	<u>V</u>. All these Treatments together.
	
	No of Sick = 76
		pmg.
		
		/–

No. 4 Field Ambulance

Capacity — Officers 8
Other Ranks 230.

	Officers		Other Ranks	
	Sick	Wnd	Sick	Wnd
In occupation	2	1	105	15
Lying	–	–	2	6
Sitting	–	–	4	6
Walking	–	–	–	–
Unfit to move	–	–	–	–
Not for evacuation	2	1	99	3

8 am
29/12/14

P.H. Clayfor[?]
Capt. R.A.M.C.
O.C. 4th Fd. Amb.

A.D.M.S.
1st Army Corps.

Nos Field Ambulance

Capacity on Arrival 8
Other Ranks 240

	Officers		Other Ranks	
	Evacuated	Held	Evacuated	Held
On occupation	2	1	10 ct	16
Lying			2	6
Sitting			8	6
Walking			—	—
Unfit to move			—	—
Held for evacuation	2	1	9	4

Korea
29-12-51

P. A. Lloyd Jones
Capt RAMC
C.O. 1 Field Ambulance

No 4 Field Ambulance

Capacity -- Officers 8
             Others 280

	Officers		Other Ranks	
	Sick	Wnd	Sick	Wnd
In occupation	2	1	86	12
Lying	-	-	Nil	4
Sitting	-	-	5	5
Walking	-	-	-	-
Unfit to move	-	-	1	1
Not for evacuation	2	1	81	2

P.A. Lloyd

Capt n Ramc
OC No 4 Field Amb

Army Form C. 2118.

WAR DIARY
or
INTELLIGENCE SUMMARY.
(Erase heading not required.)

Instructions regarding War Diaries and Intelligence Summaries are contained in F.S. Regs., Part II and the Staff Manual respectively. Title pages will be prepared in manuscript.

Hour, Date, Place	Summary of Events and Information	Remarks and references to Appendices
December 30th/14 BETHUNE	Awards a/Sergt. Hallmen, Private Banger, Private Owen, Private Marshall } awarded the Distinguished Conduct Medal. Non/Sick = 49	MJ9

No 4 Field Ambulance.

Capacity – Officers – 8
Other Ranks 280

	Officers		Other Ranks	
	Sick	Wnd.	Sick	Wnd.
In occupation	2	1	93	25
Lying	–	–	–	6
Sitting	–	–	5	11
Walking	–	–	–	–
Unfit to move	–	–	–	2
Not for evacuation	2	1	88	8

8 am
30/12/14.

C. H. L. Cooper
Capt. R.A.M.C.
O.C. 4th Fd. Amb.

D.D.M.S.
1st Army Corps.

No 11 Field Ambulance

Capacity - Officers 8
         Other Ranks

	Officers		Other Ranks	
	Sick	Wnded	Sick	Wnded
On occupation	2	1	89	22
Lying			1	7
Sitting			6	10
Walking			-	-
Unfit to move			-	-
Fit for evacuation	2	1	82	23

P. A. Lloyd Jones
Capt. RAMC
OC 11th Fd Amb

11-50 a.m.
30-12-14

O i/c
1st Army Corps

95

4th Field Ambulance

Capacity – Officers 8
Other Ranks 213

	Officers		Other Ranks	
	Sick	Wnd	Sick	Wounded
On occupation	2	–	102	24
Lying			1	4
Sitting			1	6
Walking				
Unfit to move				
Fit for evacuation	2	–	100	11

A L(?) Jones
Capt RAMC
O.C. 4th Fd Amb

5.30 p.m.
30-12-14

DMS
4th Army Corps

Army Form C. 2118.

WAR DIARY
or
INTELLIGENCE SUMMARY.

(*Erase heading not required.*)

Hour, Date, Place	Summary of Events and Information	Remarks and references to Appendices
December 31/14 BETHUNE	Very few wounded men are coming to the dressing station, but the majority of them are serious wounds inflicted by rifle (Snipers) at short range. There are a larger proportion than usual of head injuries.	[signature]

No 4 Field Ambulance.

Capacity - Officers - 8
Other Ranks - 280.

	Officers		Other Ranks	
	Sick	Wnd	Sick	Wnd.
In occupation	2	1	105	22
Lying		1		7
Sitting			4	9
Walking				
Unfit to move				3
Fit for evacuation	2		101	8

Fam
31/10/17

Capt RAMC
Off. Comm. 4 Amb

D.D.M.S.
4 Army Corps

No 4 Field Ambulance

Casualty — Officers 8
Other Ranks 280

	Officers		Other Ranks	
	Sick	Wounded	Sick	Wounded
In occupation	2	1	77	8
Dying			–	2
Sitting			1	–
Walking			–	–
Unfit to move			–	2
Fit for evacuation	2	1	92	4

~~One Officer wounded Lt 2 a.m. letters to be forwarded, with extra supplies provided, as to fit in a Hp Cord Train present for transport after all. P.A Lloyd Jones~~

11-30 a.m.
31-12-14   P.A Lloyd Jones Capt R.A.M.C
                    O.C 4 Fd Amb.

A.D.M.S.
1st Army Corps.

No 4 Field Ambulance

Capacity – Officers 8
Other Ranks

	Officers		Other Ranks	
	Sick	Wounded	Sick	Wounded
In occupation	2	1	72	14
Lying		1		1
Sitting			5	5
Walking			-	-
Unfit to move				2
Not for evacuation	2		67	6

P. H. Lapopore
Capt R.A.M.C.
O.C. 4. Fd Amb.

5-20 p.m.
31-12-14

A.D.M.S.
1st Army Corps.

Army Form C. 2118.

WAR DIARY
or
INTELLIGENCE SUMMARY.
(Erase heading not required.)

Hour, Date, Place	Summary of Events and Information	Remarks and references to Appendices
December 4/14 BETHUNE	The Operating Theatre of the Civil Hospital was put at our disposal, & after treatment is conducted in the French wards. M. Henry the Head Surgeon here is kindness itself & our associate Robert Lovett in this operation. Lieut. J. Lovell (S.C.) F RES has taken over charge of the Surgical wards and operates. Operations of importance ① For fractured Skull — Fragments removed & involved & Skull examined. ② Operation for injury to Lord. with Bone Interval Haemorrhage — This was only done 6 yrs for the Patient had lost Chance — The Secondary Chloro was then almost though the whole of its Course.	[signature]

Army Form C. 2118.

WAR DIARY
or
INTELLIGENCE SUMMARY.
(Erase heading not required.)

Hour, Date, Place	Summary of Events and Information	Remarks and references to Appendices
December 3/4/14 BETHUNE	(3) Laparotomy. — Ileo-Colostomy & resection of Ileum. — multiple wounds in Gut — The man was already moribund when operated upon. Many other minor operations such as amputations, extractions of Bullets, have been carried out since Success in various portions of the body.	PMG